This Is
**Woman's
Work**

This Is
Woman's
Work

Calling forth your inner council of wise, brave, crazy, rebellious, loving, luminous selves

DOMINIQUE CHRISTINA

sounds true
BOULDER, COLORADO

Sounds True
Boulder, CO 80306

This work is solely for personal growth and education. It should not be treated as a substitute for professional assistance, therapeutic activities such as psychotherapy or counseling, or medical advice. In the event of physical or mental distress, please consult with appropriate health professionals. The application of protocols and information in this book is the choice of each reader, who assumes full responsibility for his or her understandings, interpretations, and results. The author and publisher assume no responsibility for the actions or choices of any reader.

All etymological quotations are taken from *Webster's New Twentieth Century Dictionary Unabridged,* second edition (UK: William Collins–The World Publishing Company, 1979).

Cover design by Lisa Kerans
Cover image © Charles Bibbs, "The Gift 5"
Book design by Beth Skelley

Printed in the United States of America

BK06718

ISBN: 9781649631251

The Library of Congress has cataloged the hardcover edition as follows:
Dominique Christina.
This is woman's work : calling forth your inner council of wise, brave, crazy, rebellious, loving, luminous selves / Dominique Christina.
   pages cm
   ISBN 978-1-62203-494-9
   1. Self. 2. Women--Psychology. I. Title.
   BF697.D646 2015
   155.3'33--dc23
                              2015005859

Ebook ISBN 978-1-62203-562-5

10 9 8 7 6 5 4 3 2 1

Dedicated to my mother, Jacquelyn Benton, who is the widest example of woman I have ever known.

Contents

an introduction

Our Unclaimed Hallelujahs

Why is it important for women to define themselves? While it is important for everybody, everywhere, to do that work, for me, there is an urgency for women. When you have inherited a construct that names, describes, and practices out an ideology that women are somehow less important, less necessary, then the work of defining yourself carries with it a kind of fury—or Fury.

In Greek mythology, the Furies were three women born from the blood of Uranus, the god of sky, when his son Cronus wounded him in battle. In other words, the blood of a wounded warrior gave rise to these fiery women. The metaphor for me is luminous. In a patriarchal context (and we *are* living in a patriarchal context), the machinery that often drives politics oppressive to women is borne out of a wounded warrior motif and the inheritance of war that passes between father and son. I have long believed that if men had not been conditioned to be conquerors, then women would not need to be a regarded as a designated underclass. To that end, one might argue that, on some level, in order for women to have authorship of themselves, they often travel through the fire, through the bloody constructs that have been built by wounded warriors.

The Furies were imagined as hags, storm-bearers, replete with serpents for hair and bat wings. They are often written as monstrous and venomous. But what the Furies were catalyzed by was a profound sense of justice. The Furies meted out punishment to those who had committed wrong swiftly and often severely. They were unapologetic about tormenting a tormentor. The murderer was punished, the destroyer of

1

family was punished, and the one who pillaged and plundered was punished for causing so much wounding. They were strong women insisting on justice and operating in the full utility of their magic. They showed up big and were unapologetic about seeking balance when wrong had been done.

The Furies also, and perhaps more importantly, represent the ways in which the nature of goddesses can be so riotously misrepresented and why being a goddess/woman requires us to author ourselves. The Furies show us *Woman,* in all of her complicated and necessary forms.

As a child attracted to mythology, I was drawn to particularly stories about "ruined" women—women we were not supposed to revere, women we were supposed to loathe, fear, or pity. Women like Medusa, an extraordinarily beautiful woman whose affinity for herself had to be met with punishment. Poseidon raped beautiful Medusa in Athena's temple, and when Medusa spoke of her violation, angry Athena transformed her into the snarling monster with serpents for hair. I've never loathed Medusa; I empathized with her. I saw countless examples of her in my neighborhood. In the same way, I never feared the Furies; I respected them. Oh, how I wish *they* had lived in my community when I was a little girl. They would have known what to do about the battering husbands that peopled my block, the little girls who refused to be authored by any hand other than their own and so were punished. How I wish there were fierce, modern-day justice-driven goddesses who could strike down the Poseidons and Athenas who lived in the neighborhood I matriculated from—goddesses who could call down the thunder and magically restore the Medusas to their original beauty. These canonical examples of fiery women show not only what we are composed of, but also the ways in which we can reclaim our own fire in our own way.

Most canonized illustrations of women authored by men portray them as purveyors of evil and the downfall of man. In stories, women must *always* be punished for being too big, too beautiful, too brilliant, or too brash, for forever communing with snakes. The lesson is always the same: women like this must be reviled and feared, shunned and shuttered. Yet I am inclined to bring those women into my family and add my name to the list of those with wings and rage and a wide capacity for self-definition. They are all welcome here.

To author ourselves, to own the expanse of our voices and our stories, is critical for us as women. We are the utterance of so many unclaimed hallelujahs rushing suddenly forth to bear witness to the birthing of our names. Many of us, by virtue of birth order, or demographic or cultural identifiers, or societal expectation nonsense, negotiate a context that asks our voices to be softer, our beauty to be dim. To regain access to our wide and widest selves, we must recognize that our identities are supposed to be in our handwriting. The only permission you need comes from you.

How do we do all of this magical transformational work? It's not so easy. I know that. In order to (re)create and define yourself, you first have to *know* yourself. Not the "you" that was handed to you by your parents, your community, your friendships, your schools and communities, your lovers, your spouses. I am talking about the complete you that can only be accessed by an inward journey.

This getting to know yourself might sound like metaphysical hooey, but it is, in fact, a stunning act of bravery. It is no small thing, the business of knowing yourself. Because women show up in the world in myriad ways. And like the Furies, we have many different, complicated, and sometimes contradictory forms; we have been misappropriated and misnamed from the outside and from the inside. And to fully know yourself is to reckon with *all* of these forms, all of these incarnations of womanness—to embrace, finally, the community of women that lives in all of us. For me, that journey necessitated that I identify myself for myself. That is what I hope this book can guide you to do.

This book is seeking to inspire wider conversations about womanness and the authorship of the self. For me, clarity came most profoundly when I took an aerial view of the feminine template as *I* had experienced it, and I acknowledged that there were observable patterns of behavior that kept showing up for me and for the women in my life.

When I studied Jungian psychology, I was fascinated by what Carl Jung had to say about archetypal behavior and how instructive it can be. I also noticed that his treatment of these archetypes did not quite capture all that I had either seen or been. Therein begins the reckoning. I do work well with thinking about these archetypes; these ways of knowing, these ways of positioning ourselves on the planet, what purposes they serve and in what ways they can hinder us.

I started naming them for myself about ten years ago. At first, the list was a comfortable one. I was deliberate about avoiding ones that caused me discomfort, either because they seemed to be anathema to what I thought I wanted to validate, or because they represented an old wound for me. But then it changed. If my truth was that I, as a woman, am vast and comprised of much, then to limit my interaction to just some of their many forms, in the interest of being "right" about things, was counterproductive and hypocritical. I couldn't live with that. So I made myself more available to the conversation.

Part of how I accomplished that was to think about things empathetically and to pay greater attention to the things that created dis-ease for me, and to try to hunt down *why* my response was what it was. Before I knew it, I was dealing in the repressed parts of my psyche. I had also inherited some languageless self-loathing that I did not even know was there until I dug a bit and risked the discomfort. Reckoning with the archetypes changed the way I came to view myself and define myself, because I saw myself in each one. Some more than others to be sure, but they were all belonging to me. That fact opened up important conversations about limiting beliefs and how predispositional thoughts can keep us from ourselves for a very long time.

Each chapter of this book introduces you to an archetype, named and described as I have come to know her. My hope is that I did not superimpose myself too much on the treatment of each archetype, but rather give them all a wide enough consideration to allow you to experience them in your own way (which is the point, really). Each chapter also includes writing exercises to help you become more acquainted with the archetype and how you interact with her.

Why writing exercises? What is it about writing that fuels an appropriate reckoning? For me, writing is a meditation. It is a form of self-expression that, when engaged deliberately, offers a way in to the parts of yourself that you are, perhaps, unaware of.

Writing also asks us to grapple with and have an intentional relationship with language. This is a critical relationship because language creates pictures in your head, and those pictures, when strung together, create a reality for you—one that you consent to. I have discovered that because so many of us do not have a deliberate relationship with language, the words we use and the pictures they create are sometimes devastating to our development. In other words, if the language I am using is designed to keep me small, then I will be small. And because I don't realize language is the carrier, I can be poised miserably in an undeclared life and participate every day in my own marginalization unknowingly.

Writing holds up a mirror. It shows you your own subconscious. In my experience, many people are interested in being right about their worldview and not having their paradigm disrupted by anything, even if the paradigm they have is damaging to them. When you write, you invite your hidden parts to dance. You invite them into the room. They start to take up space on the page. After a while, you will start to notice things about your language and even how hard you are working to not tell the *whole* truth. There is an inclination to self-protect when we are approaching the kind of clarity that can make us change our perspectives. The writing exercises are designed to help you navigate that clarity and the potential change in perspective in a way that keeps you safe, yes, but keeps you honest too.

Writing has been, for me, the thing that catalyzed my being whole, my positioning myself in the world the way I wanted to be, with real deliberation. Writing then, is about the insistence of myself, the naming of myself, the claiming of myself, and the defense of myself. So even if you do not regard yourself as a writer in the first degree, even if the writing feels a bit foreign to you, I invite you to *try anyway.*

I have not learned nearly as much about myself when I was interested only in remaining comfortable. You have all of this data about what you are like and what the world is like when you operate from comfort. You might as well find out what you are like and what the world looks like when you risk discomfort. I mean this both in terms of the inward exploration of yourself via the writing and the engaging of *all* the archetypes, especially the ones you may not have fully embraced yet.

There were things I did not know I knew until I started writing this book. For example, I was excited to write about the Rebel Woman, with whom I believed I identified with entirely, but loathe to write about the Willing Woman. The Willing Woman, for me, looked like brokenness. She looked like a white flag. She looked like a victim. Whereas the Rebel Woman looked like strength; she looked like fight. She looked like necessary resistance. And, for most of my life, she looked like me. I was certain I knew how I felt about each of them. And then I started writing, and everything changed. My absurd streak of idealism and perfectionism needed to be interrupted, and it has been. The masonry of what I believed about womanness was toppled by my willingness to look at it—all of it—another way, with another lens and a wider understanding. I'm grateful for that.

You might encounter archetypical behaviors within you that do not necessarily match up to the archetypes you thought you most identified with. And that's okay. It's better than okay—it's transformational. Let it be. Let that new awareness have residence within you. Write down what makes you most uncomfortable about the discovery. What is at risk for you if you engage this archetype? What might this new awareness teach you about yourself and how you have been processing? Remember, you cannot really have authorship of yourself unless and until you *know* yourself—and that means *all* of yourself.

If you find that there is an archetype that you don't think applies to you at all, one of two things could be happening. First, you could be in projection. Our ideas about a thing are not necessarily the reality of the thing. The only way to know for sure is to engage it fully. If you are having a big reaction to one of the archetypes, and perhaps that big reaction looks like an intense desire to avoid her, it is likely that you are operating from projection or, as was mentioned before, an old wound. But the only way to have access to the clarity is to go through the experience. It is also possible that archetypes that do not have resonance with you are more like distant cousins than sisters and mothers for you. And that's okay. You are still relative to them. We all share blood and bone with each archetype to varying degrees.

You may also have the experience of reading this book and feeling like there are some archetypes missing from the photo album of womanness *you* have come to known. And that's okay too. Remember, what is offered here is not exhaustive, but it is demonstrative of *my* experience. It should, in no way, invalidate your own. With the archetypes, I tried to capture the energy patterns that I have experienced and or observed most pervasively, with the understanding that the list is by no means exhaustive. There could easily be fifty more. We are that large, larger even. This work is about *my* truth, not necessarily *the* truth. And I offer it as a means to help you find and navigate *your* truth.

Owning your narrative requires stillness. Stillness and quietness are opportunities to empty out and to sit in that emptiness until the sound of your true voice comes flooding in, to refuse to speak until you are sure that you're doing so as *yourself.* Any time you are creating, the universe opens up to make space for you. In other words, the universe will support your efforts to define/create/author your identity. This is not meant to be romantic language, because, while things show up to support your inward journey, other things will absolutely show up to challenge it. Do not lament that. There is balance in that, and I believe in balance. Besides, in my experience, we learn more from conflict than confluence.

The art of self-creating and self-exploration is a ritual—the deepest kind if you mean it. If you're willing to be still enough. If you're willing to be empty. If you're willing to be full. If you're willing to stand in the gales of your own desires and say, "I want" and "I need." If you're willing to open your mouth and let the daylight in. Let this book be a guide. Come ready to name yourself, come with questions, come with clarity, come see what you have done with the cracking crimson of your coliseum heart.

My hope is that this book can be a tool, a useful guide, a way forward for women who are ready to spring into the fullness of themselves. My hope is that there is fire enough in you to light the altar of your heart, of your becoming.

You are invited. You are welcome. You have *always* been welcome. This is a reckoning. This is where the light is located, where the wild in you is kept. This is where the fire, your fire, your *fury,* is to be found.

one

The **Shadow** Woman

She cannot wait to be born. She is always waiting to be born.

Pulled up from dust
You are at home with secrets . . .

A nighttime quiver

A hacked up midnight

The growl we keep
In the dark and low places
We cannot bear to name

An old familiar knowing
We turn away from every morning

Shadow Woman clutching your blackness
So tight . . .

You are all that is left

Of the longing

The Shadow Woman is mostly unborn. She is the deep silence before the water breaks. Jungian psychology talks about the shadow as the unblessed or repressed parts of our personhood, the things about ourselves we do not wish to honor or integrate. For me the Shadow Woman is the secret self. The underbelly. And as pejorative as that may sound or seem, the shadow is necessary. It is what we have not yet reckoned with, but what we *must* reckon with to have full command of the self. This archetypal energy is tricky because it is purposely hidden, intentionally tucked away and guarded. It is the part of us that we gatekeep and manage. The Shadow Woman is perhaps unrealized. She is a woman in waiting. Hers may not be a fully actualized life—not yet.

If this is the holding pattern you are creating from, the thing that is at the front of the experience is silence. A silence you believe in deeply, because this silence is your home.

Some silences are inherited or bequeathed. Sometimes silences are set up for us to reside under before we are even born. Some of us live our whole lives accommodating a silence that does not serve us. But there are other silences that redeem us.

Silence in and of itself is not the equivalent of voicelessness. Voicelessness is a lockbox for which you have misplaced the keys. Silence is different. Silence is meditation. Silence is prayer. Silence is refusing to speak until you are ready, until the language is entirely your own. In my adult life I access that kind of silence all the time now. I know just where to find my own big, beautiful emptiness. I know just how to retreat to the shadows to regenerate. And I know when it is time to return to the light.

The other kind of silence, the one that hisses or insists that I should remain guarded and hidden, is far away from me now. But I remember what it felt like. I remember how I carried that silence, how seductive my closed mouth seemed after a while. This was adolescence for me. The world was noisy and possessing of too much. It was not a thing to step into. It was not safe. It was not capable of honoring me. These were the messages I played in my head the most. My secrets became the biggest parts of my personality. I was *committed* to them, to the keeping of them. My stories and my actual life were not permitted any daylight. It was a deep and solitary experience.

The payoff in this energy pattern was that there was some power I felt in remaining in the dark. The feeling that nobody really knew who I was or what my capacity was seemed a noble secret. The irony, though, was that I so envied the folks in the light. The ones who could frolic in full view. The ones who would tell you what they were and where they'd been and where they were going. What they were doing all looked so impossible, so terrifying, but so important. And I wanted that. I just didn't know how to access it. The unborn woman, the Shadow Woman, is deeply interested in her own becoming—and has deep reservations about it. She is the possessor of secrets. Mostly what I created from this energy pattern was an intricate security system and trip wire in case someone tried to *see* me.

Creating anything is about letting it be born. The Shadow Woman is seeking to move from conception to delivery. She is embryonic and undeveloped. She needs to believe that the light is hers to claim.

I think about the shadow this way: The womb is a wide and possible universe, the once and future holding place for creative energy. The ocean in our mother's belly is a reservoir of information. From there we are introduced to so much. The fragility of life. The resiliency of life. The construction of flesh and bone. The relationship we have with sound and emotion happens first in the womb. It's pretty awesome. Biology is deep. It is also instructive. And it is dark. In our mothers' bodies we are concepts, the trying-to-be-born business of being. We are, by definition, a creation story. Holding onto our bodies by holding onto her body, we are learning even then that being born requires agreement between the artist and the art. The shadow is where we first begin having this conversation with ourselves. Are we ready to be born? Have we outgrown this place, or is there more sustenance we need to glean in the dark before we step into our own becoming? It is not a place to revile. It has its purpose. Everything that was ever born grew itself in the dark.

This analogy announces itself to me, a fledgling gardener, constantly. We bury seeds in the body of (Mother) Earth and ask them to take root there. We do not expect to see them again until they have first gathered enough moxie and nurturing to emerge in the light as a new and ever possible, flowering thing. Some never poke their heads up from the dark.

In this same context, the Shadow Woman is also in the dark, mostly hidden. But make no mistake. This woman is composed. She is the ninja. And I would never posit that *everyone* is supposed to be in the "light." Darkness has its place. This position contradicts what Jungian psychology opines about the shadow. Jung reasoned that the shadow embodies latent chaos and trouble, that it is an unblessed, repressed, unconscious space of being. It is languaged, by a Jungian standard, as principally negative and problematic. I am, myself, more available to the idea that darkness can grow beauty. That it is not merely the stuff of nightmares and things that need repair. I like imagining it as a possible place. An unmapped place. A place that asks for the soul to increase. It is an unseen place. An enveloped place. A birthing place.

In the womb, in the shade of a woman's body, is where we first learn of our capacity to grow, to become something sturdy. I don't find anything negative or repressed about that. Nor do I believe that kind of deliberately veiled existence presupposes an unconscious life. In fact, it is more consistent to my understanding about growth and development that the shadow can be a source of *higher* consciousness—an awakening consciousness. In the dark there is only you. It can be the first centering place, where the flowering of your being first happens.

If the Shadow Woman is out of balance, then perhaps she *is* living an "unblessed" life—an "unconscious" life. In this context she can show up as an unintentionally hidden thing. She could be fearful of stepping into herself. Her personhood is cloaked and unborn. She may not believe she should be available to being seen. She may not have been permitted an actualized life. She may never have seen it in practice. Or perhaps if she did, she saw it mistreated or mishandled and so tucked herself into the dark and thought it a safer existence.

Attributes

- Secret-keeping
- Hidden
- Undeveloped
- Waiting
- Patient
- Guarded
- Silent

Exercise for the Shadow Woman in Balance

You are deep inside of yourself. Deep, so deep, that it is hard to find you. From here, write a birthing story—*your* birthing story.

Begin inside the inside—in the dark. Describe that darkness and what it concretizes about you. How it nourishes you. How it feeds what you are becoming. Treat it as an in-uterine treatise.

Give language to the embryonic self. What would an unborn child say from the inside? How would they describe the darkness they reside in? For example: "I don't need my eyes yet. Not here. There are waves trying to be oceans. I am becoming a new thing from the inside. Learning how to breathe salt water. Darkness is a holy thing. I am trembling and learning these bones . . ." What you write does not need to be overly sentimental, unless that is your true experience and expression.

You're writing about the chrysalis as the caterpillar sees it. You can get a jumpstart on it by trying a kick-starter line. Here are a few to consider:

- I grow best when no one is watching.
- This is the shadow. It holds me gentle.

- I live here, in the rumbling restless dark.
- Do you know me? The woman who moves
  as the moon moves?
- It is a difficult thing, being born.
- I am evidence of a fruitful midnight.
- A lesson in how to conquer your fear
  of the dark . . .
- Silence is the biggest room in the house.
- What the light does not know about me . . .
- Hurry! Hurry! Step right up! See the
  unborn woman!

If none of the kick-starter lines work for you, find your own recipe. There is a lot of room to communicate the idea of the shadow. Pick the way that is the truest representation of how *you* carry it. It is your experience. Own it.

Exercise for the Shadow Woman Out of Balance

Describe the thing that keeps you in the shadows—or keeps you silent. (This can also be the thing that keeps your ideas, your true personality, your gifts from being born.)

Now assign this thing a character. For example: "My silence is kept by a man with too many keys. He is always closing the door I am trying to walk through. He never permits my entrance. His mouth is always snarling. He has too many teeth. He never remembers my name." Describe as much of this character as you can, and remember that the "character" is the thing that keeps you in the shadows, keeps you from being "born." What do they look like? What does their voice sound like? Does it remind you of anything? What do they have on? Do they have a smell? Describe their hands, how they stand, what they look like when they walk into a room.

This exercise is one I use a lot because in describing the thing that keeps you hidden, you get to have full access to it. You get to see it for what it is; you get to recognize your relationship to it. And once you do that, you can make changes.

Examples of This Archetype

Emily Dickinson represents this archetypal energy for me. We know that Dickinson was a woman who led a mostly solitary life. A woman who kept her thoughts and ideas and ruminations to herself. Writing everything down, she crafted volumes of poetry that she did not let into the world. When she died, the world "discovered" how mighty her voice had been, and marveled over her commitment to keeping that mighty voice entirely to herself. To me, as I read about Dickinson and the poetry that poured from her, it seems that she extracted something powerful in being fairly hidden. I imagine that some aspect of her personality surely knew that what she was generating was big and necessary, but my, how she kept it close! Her commitment to remaining in the shadows makes her posthumous explosion into our awareness all the more fascinating. Her writing was her own. She offered it to no one. Her "birth" happened for the rest of us, after her death.

She has always been a fascinating figure for me. I picture her in an easy chair, emptying her soul out on paper. Gazing at what emerged, perhaps a slight smile on her face. Pleased and maybe afraid of all that universe in her body. Best to keep all that planetary wonderfully close.

two

The **Ghost** Woman

Why you hangin' 'round here, woman?
Ain't nobody taught you how to stay gone?

Ghost Woman

They will say you are a story
Nobody has business believing in
What with Jesus and integration.

How the midnight caterwauling
Is some far off whistling train
They couldn't catch if they wanted to . . .

And they don't want to.

They would rather watch the sun
Be swallowed up by God
Than to imagine you back
And creeping low 'round the basement
Shooing birds out the attic.

You are an unwanted visitor
A locked door that won't stay closed.
The hinges creak and
We are an abandoned church.
A faithless vacancy
Knocks in our chests.

We don't like a good-bye.
We are scared of resurrection.

Ghost Woman, if you can come back . . .
In your dirt-bitten don't nobody want you
Bloodless body
If you can come back hissin' through the floor boards
Grindin' your teeth,
If you can come back
Bringing the cold dead air . . .

Who can't?
Oh lord . . .
Who can't?

The Ghost Woman does not know that she is supposed to be a finished thing. To borrow from Maya Angelou, the Ghost Woman understands that "every good-bye ain't gone." She is the waymaker. She knows how not to leave. This is different from not knowing how to leave. The Ghost Woman is an "in spite of" not a "because of." For all intents and purposes, she should, in fact, be gone. There have been things that could have authored her destruction. But she did not make space for that conclusion. Consider this: she is the woman who was the flat line. The one who hovers betwixt and between here and wherever "there" is.

My grandfather used to talk about "haints" as folk who could not agree to leave, despite being pushed out of their bodies. Despite circumstances that snatched and tore at them, they stayed. The Ghost Woman is still here. Something was set up to keep her from enduring, but she is not constructed in a way that will allow her to exit. She is often baffled by the idea that she does not belong. It doesn't make sense to her that she should leave.

I experience this energy pattern as having big seismic connections to key people in her world. She cannot abandon her post. She doesn't need to feel connected to her own body so much as she needs to feel connected to others. She is, in fact, so unattached to her body at times that she cannot recognize shifts within it. She is spirit without the necessity of form. She is the woman who never really feels like her body gives her much useful data with respect to her identity or her relationships. Her spirit is where she goes to get that information. She is better than most at ignoring the sensory-based world in favor of a more spiritual one.

One of the dangers here of being so unattached to the body is that you are not in receipt of the information the body is giving you. Disease and dis-ease can fester and run within this archetypal energy. Your throat can be cut, and you will not resolve yourself to the outcome. Your lungs can collapse, and you will find some other way to breathe. You have been poisoned, but you do not care about the arsenic. Your principle concern is the people you feel intensely connected to, whether that connection is deep, abiding love or resentment. The Ghost Woman obligates herself entirely to those feelings. Those feelings tell her to stay.

If this is the energy pattern you are existing in or trying to create from, the thing at the front of it is obligation—massive, all-encompassing obligation. The Ghost Woman is unwilling to let anything pull her away from her post, her responsibilities. And my truth is that those responsibilities are governed by deep love for another (or others) or the polar opposite, which can show up as deep resentment/anger/hatred. When you try to create something with obligation informing the view, what you produce may not be entirely your own. It may be a borrowed thing.

For me, this was a space I occupied right after I gave birth to my children. I felt it most profoundly after the birth of my twins. I could not recognize my body as my own for more than a year. I felt so disengaged from it. That's extraordinary, considering how there are so many women who talk about feeling *more* connected to their bodies during pregnancy and after, if they are breastfeeding. I had the opposite experience. I felt this grand severing when I was pregnant. It felt like a hostile takeover for me. I couldn't recognize when I had to go to the bathroom sometimes. It was difficult to distinguish pain from other sensations. I was clumsy and uninvolved with my body. She was doing things I simply did not understand.

What I did understand was that I felt incredibly connected to my mother. I needed her, and it felt like I needed her all the time. I had dreams of her being taken from me somehow, and I would wake up feeling terrible sadness and fear. When I went into labor with the twins, my grandfather was still alive at the time, and he stood in the room watching me have these back-busting contractions. I just kept watching *Young and the Restless.* Pain was difficult to record. I was disconnected from my body. I did not know my body. It was not my body.

When those babies burst through me, though, they were mine. I felt a roar go up my back. I knew I would never leave them—not for any reason. I bled a lot. I had to get patched up. I remember vomiting right after delivery. I remember my breasts were leaking. And I remember not being able to plug into any of it in a real way.

It would take more than a year before my body and I started speaking to each other again. I remember that time being a period of real stagnation for me in terms of writing. A woman's body is an ever-changing continent of possibilities. She is our most persistent friend, and yet she changes so radically that at times she can be unrecognizable. I had bled and stretched and died just to get my children here. Once they were, my body had to reimagine herself as something more substantive, more sturdy, and, ironically, more tender too. After labor and delivery, my body had to figure out what this new awareness was and how it was going to function from it. I remember trying hard to write in my journal and being unable to consider language as important when there was a sink full of dishes or onesies I needed to wash or diapers I needed to change or a breast pump I needed to attach myself to. I didn't have consciousness enough to write a poem. My creation stories in this hold-ing pattern were very literally my children. I created them. That was all I could manage at the time.

That is *my* connection to the Ghost Woman archetype, but there are so many versions of this experience. The Ghost Woman can be unat-tached to her own body but entirely attached to another. She does not let pain or science stop her. Even though logic says she should be gone, her reality is different. She is insistent on the being and the staying, in spite of whatever challenges them.

The Ghost Woman has to be careful. She can experience things that make her feel like the unwanted one. People are not always in cel-ebration of this particular kind of resilience. This kind of resilience is frightening. It doesn't know how to expire or cease. In the West we so need a beginning, a middle, and an end. Our linear processing tells us that a good-bye is, in fact, gone. But sometimes we love bigger than logic. Sometimes we feel things way past reason. Sometimes we keep coming back. Over and over again we come back. We move whatever bramble out of the way. We intend to be with those connections. We intend to stay. For the Ghost Woman, exit doors look much like trap-doors, and she does not have a relationship with departures.

This could also be the woman who is in a relationship that does not honor her. She may, in fact, be perpetually harmed by it. But my God, she loves hard. She doesn't know how to do it any other way. If she tells you she loves you, she means it all her life. She will not leave you just because her flesh has expired. She will dig her heels into this life. She may not even keep any muscle memory of what physical pain feels like. She is uninterested in that anyway. But for her, emotional pain is the razor's edge. She cannot leave the people she loves. Not even if where they reside is a crime scene. Not even if her own beat up body is buried there. She stays. Or she returns. She always returns. She never really leaves. Her body is not her home. She loves the same way she loathes—like a brushfire, burning.

Attributes

- Resilience
- Obligation
- Difficulty relating to the body
- Intense attachments to relationships and/or people

Exercise for the Ghost Woman

Get somewhere quiet. You will need to spend some time getting into your body. For the Ghost Woman, this is neither easy nor convenient. Take twenty minutes just to sit still. Keep both feet flat on the floor. Take deep cleansing breaths until you can hear what that wind sounds like in your chest.

Think about your hands. Think about them until you feel them—really feel them. If you are really connecting with your body, you will begin to feel them tingle because you are acknowledging them. They respond to that acknowledgment by becoming familiar to you. Think about your hands until you start to feel their stories. The babies they held or did not hold. Their ability to carry, to comfort, to express.

Next think about your feet. Think about them until they tingle in acknowledgment of you. Then think about how they've served you. Where they took you. What they kept you from.

Continue thinking about each part of your body until you are actively engaging your whole body in conversation. Feel everything. Even the things that hurt. Perhaps *especially* the things that hurt. Pain is instructive. You are far away from your body because you have stopped listening to her.

Tell her thank you. Say it over and over again. Say it until you feel her receive the applause. Say it until she believes you. To borrow from poet Sierra DeMulder, "Your body is the house you grew up in." This is necessary housework. You are sweeping the cobwebs out. You are opening the curtains.

When you are done, write a letter to your most ignored part. This can literally be anything—your feet, your heart, your eyes, your head.

Just write a letter to the part of you that has gone most unknown, the part you feel furthest from. It is a love letter. An opus. A way to say thank you. A way to reconnect. To ask for forgiveness. And if necessary, Ghost Woman, a way to introduce your body to your spirit. They should at least be on speaking terms.

Examples of This Archetype

In the literary world, the best example is the character Beloved in Toni Morrison's novel of the same name. Beloved is absolutely a ghost woman. She could not commit to leaving. She is, in essence, a child whose need for the mother was so great that even *after* her mother cut her throat to keep her from experiencing chattel slavery, this child's clamoring was so significant that it allowed her to re-inhabit a body in order to be joined again with her mother.

Nothing about our world readily supports such a notion. And yet, in the Christian tradition, the centralizing figure is *himself* a man who defies death more than once. Even if you read the Bible as literature and not scripture, you have to reckon with Lazarus's resurrection (as facilitated by Jesus) and Jesus's transmogrifying one.

Maya Angelou has it right: every good-bye ain't gone. Popular films like the movie *Ghost* also present the idea that, despite what we may believe, a person can exit their body and be unaware of that experience. They can still identify with their right now life. They can operate in defiance of reason or science if their attachments or obligations are big enough. The Ghost Woman is willing to haunt every room. And she probably does not even recognize it as a haunting.

three

The **Willing** Woman

She a closed mouth. She a yes every time.

For "N"

You squattin' down under
a clanging life with too loud
a man in it, look around and
all your parts are scattered
'cross the living room like you forgot
what dancin' felt like and it takes you
so many mornings
to collect all the broken
syllables in your name,
each mishandled moment
that made your bones
sit in your body
like canons,
like war,
like thrumming from the inside
wouldn't eventually kill you,
like your mama didn't tell you about your magic
before you struck a match
between her thighs.
And now all you know is your shut mouth.

Don't have enough teeth to chew through

the bloody stumped memories.

You want to climb the sky but

can't find your throat no place

everything is a bottled up capture

can't no light get inside the way you love

cuz you love like a lynchin' rope,

like a wound,

like a dead thing,

like a broad stroke,

you love like a trench,

gobblin' up the night . . .

lawd your own sunken self

is peekin' up through bolted door

wantin' to know somethin'

about the outside

if you could get your limbs back

if you could get your limbs back . . .

you could get up . . .

you might could get free.

The Willing Woman is available. She is what I imagine feminism hates the most. More than patriarchy or misogyny, the woman who is obedient is the "problem." The woman who does what she is told. The woman who does not talk back or speak out. The woman who is not interested in fighting back or saying no. The woman who is willing to defer. Willing to submit. Willing to serve and obey and offer and follow instructions and obey and obey and obey.

I'm not going to lie. I struggle with her. In my mind, she is not interested in winning. She is not interested in much about herself.

But I think I am wrong. I think my perspective may be too narrow and judgmental to hit the mark just right. Even in my struggles with this particular presentation in the world, I know I am wrong about the Willing Woman if I am trying to describe her as a spineless woman or a woman without dreams and ideas for herself. That is not a true depiction.

I have a very deliberate relationship with language. I don't want to believe I know what I am saying or what words actually mean; I want to *know* that I know. It is in this capacity that I want to explore the idea of the obedient or Willing Woman archetype.

Let's look at the word *obey* etymologically. That always grounds my awareness—and deepens it.

> obey (v.) late 13c., from Old French *obeir* "obey, be
> obedient, do one's duty" (12c.), from Latin *obedire,*
> *oboedire* "obey, be subject, serve; pay attention to, give
> ear," literally "listen to," from *ob* "to" (see ob-) + *audire*
> "listen, hear"

I will start with what I am challenged most by: the idea of being subject. This for me invokes a conversation around inferiority. This person in my mind is operating from an inferior position, a powerless position. Because of how I am wired both politically and emotionally, I want to posit that this person is not in full command of her experiences. She is at the whim and/or mercy of another.

The most basic example is a child. Where they are going is not up to them. How they get there is not up to them. What they are doing and at what speed and for whom is not really up to them. Theirs is a directed and mandated life. A governed life. A regulated rule-driven life. We preside over children because we believe they need it. We do not believe that they are able to manage themselves autonomously. Thusly, they oblige themselves to our precedence because that is the nature of how things between children and adults are set up. And because there are things that support the idea that we know more than they and that guidance is what they need and what we can offer.

When we mature and come into ourselves, my truth tells me that such a position is no longer appropriate, no longer necessary. If, as an adult, you are still obliging yourself to an obedient life, my default setting is to deem that problematic because it looks like powerlessness to me, which I am vehemently opposed and unattracted to.

Here's the thing though: Can't it be argued that making the choice to show up in service and obeisance is a kind of power? If we put this idea in a religious or spiritual context, don't most traditions and practices suggest that surrender and obedience is, for the believer, the most powerful place one can stand? The abandonment of the ego in favor of vulnerability and availability to guidance—isn't that what faith asks?

I am not trying to have a theological conversation at all, but I am looking for an alternate perspective, a wider, more open-minded perspective. Why do I project that everyone should have power, and why do I believe that I have the only right ideas about what that power is and is not? Isn't power about choice? Isn't power about understanding what you are composed of and being able to access what you need? What if what you need is to obey? What if what you need is to be in service, to be the person who says yes most often? What if what you need is to be the person whose contentment is perhaps derived from being told what you need to do and having the capacity to do it? It's still tricky for me, but I think I'm on to something. If feminism or womanism cannot make space for the willing/obedient woman, how are feminism/womanism really about a woman's right to herself? What if what she wants is to obey? And if that is what she wants, what she absolutely and authentically wants, isn't that a thing to honor? Are we certain that a woman would never actually want that, and if she does, it is because she is broken or conquered? Why are we so convinced of this?

As educators, we are constantly asking our students to be able to adhere to "the rules" in order to navigate a social stratosphere that, without those rules, could cause them harm or bring them into circumstances that threaten their ability to be whole. When our kids/students are willing to remain "obedient" even in the face of challenges, it is, for all intents and purposes, a *powerful* place to stand.

And to be clear, obedience is a choice. I think the caveat for me is to delineate when the choices are coming from a person who chooses to obey or submit because it is what they really want and what they believe best honors them versus the person who chooses to obey because they don't recognize that they have another choice, because their choice is driven by fear, because the choice is wound born. The latter is, from my perspective, a broken soul. The former is a wildly different interpretation of freedom than I have ever heard feminism really allow or consider. Quite frankly, it's difficult for *me* to grapple with, but it is the kind of tension worth feeling. I do not wish to revile the Willing Woman. I know she is made of sterner stuff than her position may suggest on the surface. Obedience, then, requires a kind of power that I haven't fully reckoned with. To know you have the ability and space to do something different but to elect instead to adhere to the wishes of another is surely composed of an almost Zen-like capacity for patience and what seems to me to be an egoless experience.

I only have one reference for this in my own life. I show up big, on purpose. I am not interested in deference, not in the giving *or* receiving of it. I like being free. It affirms the ideas I have about myself. That said, when I love someone "with a love that is more than love" (thank you, Edgar Allan Poe), that person can tell me what to do, and I do it. I do it gladly too. It feels like I am offering my partner something that has real weight. I'm not being the sacrificial lamb. That's not what it feels like. It feels like I am rendering a mighty, powerful gift. If you are relative to me at all, then you have the experience of me as being someone who does (almost exclusively) what she wants to do. If I move that out of the way or, even more to the point, if what I want to do (because of my feeling for you) is what you want me to do in that moment, then it seems to me I am demonstrating real power in being able to offer that in the face of all this strong black girl/independent woman business.

Now, the opposite end of the spectrum is, of course, the woman who believes she does *not* have power or choice enough to go another route. Hers is a white-flagged position, a defeated, laid-low position. I can't celebrate this, but I do have some empathy—and perhaps even some fear. I know it can happen to the strongest kind. I know we can write ourselves into a script that has the plot constructed from our own undoing. I know this. I'm afraid of this.

There is a woman in my community who, from my lens, occupies this space right now. A wife and a mother to two small children, pregnant with her third, she is dutiful and submissive. Her husband routinely takes credit for the work *she* does. She always covers up his deficits, letting him claim authorship of her hard work. She has been doing this for years. I think her paradigm is that this is how you are supposed to love. When she found out about his infidelities, she puddled over. Sitting in shambles in my girlfriend's living room, she wept and she roared and she talked of betrayals and how dare he. When she confronted her husband, he told her that this other woman was to be his second wife and that she should simply learn to accept it because she would otherwise be a single mother. She acquiesced. She held up her white flag and stood where he told her. Now whenever I venture onto social media (and I don't that much anymore, admittedly), I see pictures of the husband with his two wives and their children—all smiling into the camera. When I look at *her*, I see all of the things she is denying about who she is and what she wants. I see a fractured image, a woman who cannot remember how abundant she is. And it makes me sad. And angry.

If the Willing Woman is the energy pattern you are holding, what is at the front end of it (if you are doing what is best for you) is service—the inclination to listen more than to be heard, the inclination to give. If the Willing Woman is the energy pattern you are holding because you cannot locate your own free will, what is at the front end of it is misconception/mythology. In other words, you are operating from the idea that you don't have any other place to stand, and that is never really true.

Attributes

- Service
- Committed listening
- Sacrifice
- Acceptance
- Or hopelessness
- Fear
- Self-loathing
- Old wounding

Exercise for the Willing Woman in Balance: Obedience as a Powerful Place to Stand

You are prolific in your ability to move yourself out of the way. To make space for another's wishes, to gather up your personhood around someone else. There is a payoff for you in doing this.

Take a moment to locate yourself in the experience of service to another. Write down five things obeisance gives you, five things—five truths—it tells you about yourself that you value. List them out. I don't think it's necessary to be overly concerned with their order.

Once you have your list, expand each item. In other words, if your first one is, "I know how to love unconditionally," explore why this is a thing of importance for you. Who showed you this aspect in your development? Or was it that you never saw it in practice and so it became a thing you cleaved yourself to?

Each item on your list should require paragraphs from you. Be diligent about naming why each one is a thing you value and from whence those ideas came. Our ability to recognize where our values come from is critical. You have set your life up according to the importance you've assigned to these things. You should know why they matter to you. Writing them down deliberately is about bringing them squarely into your awareness. Your own narrative might surprise you. You may even discover that there are things on the list that you have, in fact, outgrown or no longer really need. Or you may realize in a more concrete way why these things are the stuff of your being.

Exercise for the Willing Woman Out of Balance: Obedience as a White Flag

There is a wound somewhere. However far-flown or distant, there is a wound, and it is an old one. It is announcing itself by way of your interactions, your relationship(s). Here is where you have an opportunity to stare into that wound—and to know that looking into it will not kill you.

I want you to identify when you first felt a real sense of powerlessness. When did it come online? Who showed it to you or made you feel it first? I do not want this exercise to retrigger you, and so you are going to take an aerial view of the circumstances and/or individual(s) that first made you feel powerless. Whatever skills you had then, they are more developed now. They are wider now. And there are more of them, whether you know it or not. Perhaps you have come to believe that moment told you all you needed to know about your personhood, your identity, your position in this world. And that is a lie. We are never our worst moments. It is always, *always* possible to emerge on the other side of a thing with what you need to overcome that thing.

Write a letter to the person you were when you first felt helpless. Tell her about how beautiful and necessary she is. Tell her about the gaping hole she leaves in the universe by disremembering her gifts, her purpose. Remind her of the things she loved once. Remind her about the stuff that made her blood move. Tell her about them with real enthusiasm. Show her all the colors. Tell her the stories of her dreams. Ask her to live there for a while. Tell her she has a right to it all.

And tell her you forgive her. For forgetting what she knew, you forgive her. For losing her way home, you forgive her. For ignoring the universe in her body, you forgive her. Tell her she can reclaim these things. Tell her these things have been waiting for her to pick her head up from the hooks of experience that hauled her spirit down to dance a freedom song. Tell her she is a freedom song. Tell her and tell her and tell her. She will listen. She will want to believe you. Tell her these things until she does.

Examples of This Archetype

The literary character that emerges for me right away is Celie in *The Color Purple*. Alice Walker writes this woman as the most obedient kind. No fight in her anywhere. She is a misused woman. Her childhood was fraught with sexual abuse. She was married off to a man she neither knew nor loved. He beat her and participated upon her without any real agreement from her. And she remained obedient—*until* she felt a fire catch in her belly. *Until* she had the expedience of another woman showing her what free could look like, what it could be like, how she could access it, and when she was ready, she found her spine to be remarkably straight. She found a roar in her bones. It was then that she resisted. She rebelled against her own fear and self-loathing, her own powerlessness and the gross misuses of power that had maimed her. And she got free.

four

The **Rebel** Woman

She a clenched fist. She gon tell you no and mean it.

She a red thing

A still thing

A you-can't-tell-me-nothin' thing
A reachin'-for-her-razor thing.

She a hollow point

A bloody mishmash

Her knapsack full
Of rumble and stomp.

She a red thing

A hot thing

A she-ain't-gon-be-moved thing
A right now red river resisting thing.

She see left and go right
She see stay and go runnin'
She hear hush and start squealin'.

She done made "no" a religion.

Two closed fists be how she worship
Two closed fists be how she worship . . .
She say amen and won't budge.

The Rebel Woman is an identity defined by juxtaposition—an identity
formed from *without*. In other words, she knows who she is by standing
against a thing. By opposing that thing. By standing on the opposite end of
that thing. By refuting that thing. Agreement is not necessarily her strong
suit. Her reality is borne out of resistance. In the interest of consistency,
let's look at the word *rebel* etymologically and see what clarity it offers.

When the word is used as an adjective to describe a person and their
behavior, its etymology is:

> rebel (adj.) c.1300, from Old French *rebelle* (12c.),
> from Latin *rebellis* "insurgent, rebellious," from *rebellare*
> "to wage war against again," from *re* "again" + *bellare*
> "wage war," from *bellum* "war."

This is instructive for me. War again. War again. And again. The Rebel
Woman has an identity that is about the perpetual fight. She is resolved
to it. She is going to jut out—on purpose. She doesn't wish to tuck into
some neat and acceptable formulaic equation. She sees the world as a
place in need of revision, redirection, redecoration. Whether that is a true
and accurate perception is up for discussion. But the rebel woman is not
content with what is, so she positions herself against it—over and over
again. She is the resister. Her trench warfare tells her what she needs
to believe/know about herself. For me it begs the question, though: Is
the Rebel Woman fighting a righteous, noble fight? Is hers a legitimate
platform? Or is she resisting for the sake of resistance? Can she distinguish between the two? I am interested in looking at it all.

I have a predilection for the rebellious archetype. I think I should be honest about that. I would posit that this predilection is connected to my cultural identity and patterns of behavior that have been held up for me as laudable ones. In an African American context, given the strange and terrible legacy of slavery, stories about those who resisted were heroic and supernatural in my eyes. So much of how I identify with being a colored girl is connected to what I have had to resist in order to step fully into that identity in a way that makes me proud.

The construct of racism offered me plenty of things to rebel against and resist. Ideologies, people, systems, institutions—all things I believed were designed to demean me, demoralize me, or otherwise make me small. Resistance was the theme, for me anyway. I am relative to those who showed up differently. To people who were, in fact, convinced they were historical bad luck accidents. To people who took our historical context in this country and let that mad history tell them they were conquered or less than.

But I never bought into the idea that I was cursed with history. I reckoned with how I originated differently. I *knew* black was not a blight. I knew I was made of much. I come from people who demonstrated consistently that we were anything but small. For me, this meant anything that suggested otherwise was a lie I was not going to languish under. I was further buoyed by examples I found of other rebellious souls who did not consent to their own destruction. Only tales of slave revolts on ships like *La Amistad* softened stories of middle-passage nightmares. The former told me how, even in the most soul-crushing circumstances, an individual can find a way to keep their spine straight, to keep their commitments to themselves. To learn (later) that there were also women who rebelled and resisted historically, and certainly also contemporarily, lifted the sky into my chest. Between racism and sexism, I had a cornucopia of reasons to raise my fist and fight.

And now the rub: resistance as habitual practice. Even more than that, resistance as an *identity* requires that a person assemble themselves as the counterargument. Rebellion is an exhausting practice. You are constantly at odds with something. When this experience is out of balance, it can be difficult to distinguish between a worthy cause and just another wrestling match. There have been times in my life when this was true, when all I knew to do was scrap and stand against. Rebellion looks like power to me. It looks like bravery. But if you are resistant or rebelling without reason, it is no longer a position of relevance. It is, in fact, a way to bleed out. Even now I am cognizant of how I am organically positioned to assume a rebellious or resistant position—in conversations, in my writing. It seems to me, when I really dig into it, that I am often writing to refute one notion or another. Sometimes it's big, sweeping political statements. Sometimes it's social commentary. Sometimes it's a deliberately constructed statement about how mighty I am, a statement I believe, but I offer it most times not because *I* need the clarity, but rather because I imagine that such a statement is standing in direct opposition to things that suggest something else.

War again and again. The perpetual resistance movement. You say left, so I am inclined to consider right. You say stop, and plans to charge ahead are already organizing themselves in my brain. I have enough years on the planet and subsequent life experiences now, though, to recognize when I am a misdirected distribution of rebellion. Sometimes the clarity comes after I have already offered my energy unnecessarily to a thing, and then when I am war-walloped and exhausted on the other side, I can see where I misappropriated my resources. The feeling that I am most myself when my fists are clenched is a thing I am trying to let go of now.

Don't get me wrong. I still revel in how mighty I feel when I stand on the other side of an old idea and call bullshit, but sometimes I crane my neck into the space the "other side" occupies and take a good look around. Sometimes I even see where they're coming from. Sometimes I can find empathy. Other times I recognize value in the opposing argument. That does *not* mean that I shift my position, necessarily, but it does allow my position to make space enough to accommodate the other one. When I can do that—when I am *willing* to do that—I feel just as mighty then too.

If the Rebel Woman is the energy pattern you are holding, what is at the front of it, in my mind, is disagreement. You are creating from dissent, from objection. Some of my most palatable poems have been written from this place. I believe that is a true statement primarily because resistance calls the thunder. It feels tectonic. I imagine myself to be Medusa in the writing. All scales and hiss and boom. Protecting what is softer and gentler about me. Jesse Jackson's sound bite phrase from the 1980s, "I am somebody!" is, in fact, the very idea I am trying to protect in my own rebellion. I am somebody. I am somebody. If patriarchy suggests otherwise, I resist. If racism suggests otherwise, I resist. If trauma suggests otherwise, I resist. I am somebody. I am somebody. That platform still calls me to action most days. And at the same time, I recognize that, most days, just my being, just the ways I insist on my *self,* advances that platform. Yes.

Attributes

- Persistent
- Savvy
- Quick-witted
- Brave
- Action oriented
- Or stubborn
- Argumentative

Exercise for the Rebel Woman

This is a simple one: For one week, practice holding the opposing position. All of the things you rally against, the things you resist the most, write them down in no particular order and take up their cause. Make a list wherein you defend each item. Be thorough, as difficult as it may be. Go all the way into the other side. Try on the other perspective.

The only danger in connecting with the thing you've been rebelling against is discovering that you might not be so invested in your position after all. And if that happens, that's not a bad thing. Growth happens by virtue of being willing to stretch your lens over and over again.

Once you have your developed list, I want you to turn it into a list poem where every line begins with "This is where my energy goes." If you are resisting a thing, as mentioned earlier, you are giving some part of your energy to that thing. Even if it is just by virtue of your consideration. By starting each line with the very literal naming of that reality, you ground the why of the fight. It is intended to offer you insight. Inevitably I discover that I am uncomfortable with much of what I've named. Not necessarily because I no longer believe in my position, but because I start to wonder, in some cases, why I offer my energy to a thing that does not deserve it.

Rebel Woman, you are all spine and heart—and these are valuable resources. You should be diligent about offering them up with a clear head. As an alternate or additional writing exercise, you can write a poem wherein you name five acts of rebellion from you. Then five lies you've told. Then five more acts of rebellion. These rebellious acts can begin in childhood. Like,

> #1. I put glue on Sister Dehlia's chair.
> #2. I lie to my mama about where the cookies went.
> Etc.

List poems are easy to step into. There is no rigid form to follow. Your list can be as whimsical or profound as you like.

Examples of This Archetype

At the risk of bringing the United States government down on my head, I say Assata Shakur is a dynamic example of the Rebel Woman. Angela Davis. Elaine Brown (look her up if she's unfamiliar). Gloria

Steinem. Nina Simone. Rosa Parks. Fannie Lou Hamer. Women who resist(ed) . . . again and again. They were deeply committed to vast political platforms and ideological stances, in spite of clear and present danger and consequence. They were the juxtaposition. They buttressed up against, spoke out, stood up, or, in the case of Rosa Parks, *refused* to move. The fight . . . again . . . and again.

five

The Woman with **Cool Hands**

She is her own medicine. A balm.
A healer. Her hands are always open.

Granny Phifer would make you
Grits and eggs til your belly
Split to smiling
Knitted socks and mittens
That never fit right
But they taught you
About gratitude and . . .

That time you swallowed
Pills in the medicine cabinet
In the basement bathroom
And collapsed
A trembling yawp
Pushed your mouth down for hours
And how
She brought her
Hands to stop
Your boiling skin
From spillin' you out
All over everything
How she cooed and
Kept time with

Every moan
How she rocked
You til your blood
Moved right in
Your body again

Her cool-weather hands
Singing the relationship
Between skin and bone . . .
She gave you your body back
Gave it right back
Like it shoulda been
Like it was meant to be

Even now when you take sick
You think of the lickety split
Whisper stroke of cool hands
And the fever breaks
It always breaks
In just the right way . . .

Just the right way

The Woman with Cool Hands is the caregiver. She is balm and bless-ing. She looks after you when you are ailing—and when you are not. She is the woman who keeps the soup pots full of wonderful. She is the cool towel on your head. She is the "can I get you anything?" woman. If you say no, she will likely bring you something anyway. She is a wide lap and an available ear. She is the Good Samaritan. Her generosity tells her she is loving in the right way. Her kind of selflessness looks like homemade cookies and a turned-down bed. It is central to her identity.

My partner is a caregiver. Denice is motivated by meeting the needs of others. It makes her feel useful. She is most comfortable when she is providing for another. She feels necessary—noble even. We had a discussion on the phone wherein she posited that I was also a caregiver, and I had to correct her. I am a mother. And in this capacity I take care of my children. But that is not what I *am*. It is merely what I *do*. There is a big distinction for me around this.

Caretaking another does not motivate me. In fact, I am probably closer to the self-seeking, self-serving category. I don't regard that as a lofty or particularly appropriate position, but it seems hardwired about me. In caring for others I meet an obligation, like a host of other obligations I meet. Paying my bills, keeping the lights on, attending meetings when I say I will—all obligations, like feeding my children and keeping a roof over their heads. The only way I feel personally connected to this archetype as it appears in me is in the inclination I have to encourage others to confront and heal from experiences that wounded them. To knuckle in around whatever is pulling them away from their best self, their widest capacity. But even in this, I think I am concerned about it because it is, at the core, necessary soul work for *me*. I benefit from peering into the abyss to exhume what's conspiring against me, to hold it up to the light, to know as much as I can about myself and my own capacity. Even in my helping others to move through the murkier parts of their experience, I am motivated by my own healing as much as (or more than) their being taken care of.

I imagine that the Woman with Cool Hands is different. Her relational strength is rooted primarily in service and being comfort to others. In a patriarchal culture this can be squelched down and misinterpreted as a kind of weakness. I have heard the caregiver archetype mischaracterized as the martyr. Perhaps if she is out of balance, that is how it can manifest itself. If she is wounded and suffering in service so that others might be made whole or redeemed in some way, then yes, her caretaking can look like martyrdom. Martyrdom *is* the intricate relationship between service and suffering. I imagine that this aspect would be the consequence of a wounded, unfocused caretaker. She might be or become challenged by the idea of self-care. She cannot remember how to pour into herself. She is meeting the needs of others above her own.

But I do not believe that the Woman with Cool Hands necessarily operates from this place. The woman who cared for my great-grandfather was not a martyr. The woman who cared for my grandfather was not a martyr. My girlfriend is not a martyr. The women I am relative to who hold this energy pattern show up large. They have very clear ideas about who they are and how they intend to show up in the world. And their model of service is not synonymous with suffering. They deal in empathy and good deeds. They deal in connection, and much of that connection is in their ability to be necessary and useful to others. It is not a low position. It is, in many respects, a healing one.

Now, there is a relevant conversation around this energy pattern when the person being "cared for" is not interested in that. The caregiver needs to be needed. I imagine that it is discomfiting and jarring for her to negotiate a person who is resistant to being cared for. In this context, the caregiver looks like a pest. A woman insistent on bringing you a plate of food though you told her you just ate. When you rebuff her or refuse what she is offering, the Woman with Cool Hands is sometimes offended or saddened by it. She needs to give you what she has. The relationship depends on your accepting it. In this regard, it is important for the woman who occupies the caregiver's space to be able to take a step back.

Woman with Cool Hands, your gift is in your selflessness. Your graciousness. Your care. Where you might falter is in trying to insist on giving to someone who is not interested in receiving or in failing to remember to take care of *yourself*. When you are trying to create from this archetypal pattern, what you offer to the world is very literally *for* the world. Whatever you are generating is probably a thing you think others need to see or hear or connect with. You are creating as a way to gift others, to offer them what you think they need.

This is also how I know I am not principally a caregiver. Every single aspect of my creative process is for *me;* it's what *I* need. If the world benefits from it, I am delighted by it, but I am not driven toward that outcome. That is not what moves my pen. That is not why I do what I do. Self-sacrifice is not something I am particularly good at. My girlfriend is also a writer. My experience of her work is that much of it is about offering *us* something. In some cases what she is offering is an opportunity for us to change, to shift our views about a thing.

Attributes

- Selfless
- Attentive
- Generous
- Healing presence
- Altruistic
- May struggle with self-care

Exercise for the Woman with Cool Hands

You love with your arms out, woman. You love in service. You love in offerings. Write a poem in second person. Write it in the form of the childhood "see Spot run" books. Write a list of things you do to care for others. It can read like this: "See Dominique. She is in the kitchen. Cook, Dominique, cook. Dominique makes cakes for her children. Her children smack their lips. Smack, children, smack. See Dominique. She is always working. Work, Dominique, work. This is how Dominique loves. She loves with her hands full. Love, Dominique, love. . . ."

If this form feels too rigid or inaccessible to you, try this: write down eight gifts you give when you love and then name how you love. Every line can be structured this way: 1. I give _____ because I love like a _____.

Try to get eight things down. The things you "give" can be literal (like time, attention, patience, loyalty), or they can be more metaphorical (like my unbowed head, the stars in my eyes).

Then get honest about naming *how* you love. For example, "I give my unbroken heart because I love like a forest fire." Or, "I give my commitment because I love like a promise." Do eight of these.

When you've finished, look at what came out of you. Are they all true statements? Was there ever a time when they were *not* true statements? What did that feel like? Does your list look like you? Would the people you caretake agree with what you wrote? Are *you* in agreement with what you wrote? Was there anything that surprised you? Anything you think should change?

I am obviously a sucker for clarity. I love the opportunity to see what is rumbling in my consciousness. To unpack it. To engage it. Take your time with this. Sit still and wait for the words to come. You have the framework. Your internal compass will show you precisely how you're positioned, cool-handed woman. You are so proficient in offering to others. But this—this is for you.

Examples of This Archetype

Mother Theresa—an obvious example, to be sure, but worth offering. The late Princess Diana seemed to me to be a caregiver. How she moved in the world did not, from my perspective, seem to be about politics. It seemed to be about a deep recognition of needs and her own inclination to meet them where and how she could. It looked to give her purpose for sure, but more than that. It looked to me like her work was important to her because it deepened *her* importance. She helped scores of people and, in so doing, became necessary to them. She was a life preserver. A shade tree.

six

The **Conjure** Woman

You got so much magic, girl, you thick with it.

Unbraided conjure woman
Lookin' for wind . . .
You ain't no ordinary anything.

They gon keep lookin' for you
To duck down under all those stories
Those lonesome hooked mouth
Tellin' lies stories
Bout you bein' small
Enough to chew through.
The words gon drop on your feet
Like a stillbirth
Like a dead thing.

Everything they ever said
Was a hollow place
To hide your body in.

But you? You keep growin'
Your body too big for holding down
They can't get the nails in just right.

You a magic thing.
Keepin' lemon balm and lightning bugs.

49

Your sharp straight neck
Your biting teeth.
Your unsplit womb
Your mud-struck life
You are a dance conjure woman
Your knuckles shook loose
Your pushed out knees
You a slow sizzle conjure woman.

You look like the old ones
The fire and cauldron bubblin' ones
The creepin' round the darkness ones.

You a real old thing, conjure woman.

So old we forgot your name.

The Conjure Woman is deep-belly-of-the-earth woman. Ritual woman. Magic and spirit and root-worker woman. Sorceress-priestess-pastor woman. The *bruja*. The unnamed one. The oldest prayer. She is what midnight looks like. She is what dawn is trying to become. She is connected. She is frequency and rumble and pitch. The witch, though we are too often unclear about how to carry that word. She is the maker. She is her own temple, her own divining place.

In my own cultural traditions—African, African American, and certainly Native American—the Conjure Woman/the magic woman/ the *bruja* is pervasive. She is, in fact, so present in our awareness that she is sometimes regarded as rather unremarkable. Part and parcel of our everyday always life. When I read literature that originated from colored folks (and I'm using that phrase deliberately because I like it and I can), I see the Conjure Woman throughout. Of course there is a woman you can go to who will do what God hasn't gotten around to—if she even ascribes to a God. Of course she can speak to the ancestors on your behalf. Of course she has a potion, a brew, a concoction that can help you sleep or get you hitched or fix your relationship with your mama.

I know, I know. Sounds illogical in the Western world. But the Western world has its own wild relationship with magic, even if it is to threaten it, burn it at the stake, or deny its existence all together. The West does not believe in magic, but we are *afraid* of it.

I want to draw what light I can from the etymology of the word *magic*. Etymologically, *magic* is a term derived from the word for Zoroastrian priests *(magoi)* in ancient Persia, who were reputed to be great sorcerers. It is from Old Persian *magush,* "to be able, to have power." Etymologically, the word *magic,* in the late fourteenth century, meant "the art of influencing events and producing marvels using hidden natural forces."

To have power, to be able, to produce marvels using hidden *natural* forces. The Conjure Woman, the magic woman, almost sounds like a gardener. She almost sounds like a teacher. She almost sounds like a writer. A musician. An alchemist. By virtue of the etymology of *magic,* she sounds like almost every woman I know who is a mother. Hell, she sounds like almost every woman I know *period.* When are we *not* doing "the impossible"? When are we not turning nothing into something? When are we not?

My biases are showing. The Conjure Woman is paradoxical for the Western mind, and yet she exists wholly there. She is a spiritual dilemma because she exists without consent to a rigid religious context. She is her own religion. She is every religion. She is no religion at all. My friend is an atheist. She does not believe in God, but she does believe in magic—her own magic primarily, but she leaves the door open just wide enough for the possibility of other folks to be possessing of their own supernatural something. What a Judeo-Christian context calls a miracle, the Conjure Woman calls magic. Jesus, then, would be interpreted as a magician, an illusionist. This interpretation doesn't undermine his relationship to a God experience; it merely posits that one thing didn't necessarily facilitate the other. It suggests that the miracles and/or magic that was ascribed to Jesus was not because he was a deity, but because he was *connected*. My friend Faatma would assert that God had nothing to do with the whole walk-on-water, raise-Lazarus-up-from-the-dead, turn-water-into-wine business. All they took was some good strong magic and the will to make it manifest.

I have never had a problem believing in magic. In fact, a more succinct way to say it is, magic has never needed consent or agreement from me to announce itself, to be what it is. I have always known women who were composed of ritual, women who operated with no limiting beliefs in power. They knew that in order to influence something, to move or alter or change or lift up or destroy, you had to (1) be able to recognize and (2) harness the power available in life itself. "Life" as in the persistent energy on the planet—the power in nature (water, fire, earth, air) and spiritual power (spirit, soul, ancestors, God). These women knew how to have conversations with river and rock. They talked to the old ones by leaving slips of paper in glass bottles. They waded in the water til the water believed them. Women who called down the thunder. Women who rain danced. Women who could tell you your future in a pile of chicken bones. Women who never forgot their connections to spirit and spirits.

In late seventeenth-century Salem, we burned these women. We reviled them and put them on trial. Their spiritual practice was an unsanctioned spiritual practice, so we snatched at them, tied them to trees, threw their bodies to the dogs, destroyed them. Fear seems to function that way. If it is a thing we do not understand, we fear it, and once we fear it, we seem obliged to loathe it. And once we loathe it, we have to punish and destroy it. For making us confront our own dogma. For making us wonder about God. For making us reconsider what we were told is possible. We are not comfortable with paradigm shifts. We need to believe we have it right. We need to believe that our way of knowing is the only way of knowing, is the best way of knowing. So much of the isms on the planet and the subsequent violence that follows are about this mechanism. So much of it is fear and loathing because our lens is deliberately narrow.

Even as I write this, I wonder about how my Christian friends will feel, how Muslims will feel about my narrative. I am not supposed to ascribe to any of this. The most crushing and perpetual critique is that to consider the Conjure Woman and her magic as valid is to go against God. Which, quite frankly, I'm not about. But I do not agree with the assessment that the Conjure Woman is against God. The Conjure Woman can be an evangelist. She can be a preacher in a pulpit on Sundays. When she holds out communion wafers, prays over them, and then asks us to believe that the wafers are "the body of Christ," in that moment she is attempting to conjure. In that moment she is her witchiest self.

In Islam when you make *salat* (prayer) and you are folded on your knees, you are taught to keep your right index finger up. Though some scholars differ on the why of it, I was told that it was (1) because Prophet Muhammad was observed doing it, and his was an example to follow, and that (2) it was a matter of declaration of the oneness of God and exclusive devotion to Him. Ritual/conjure is not only about deepening belief. Sometimes ritual/conjure is about suspending belief in favor of magic or miracle. I'm confident I am going to get backlash for saying *that*.

I have always experienced women to be incredibly attuned to spirit. Perhaps it is because a woman's position on the planet, in terms of biology and by social construct too, is to be creators (should we elect this). A tree knows the earth better than any because it is plugged into it. She cannot bear fruit without that connection. The Conjure Woman is a root worker. She is interested in the source. She is available to it. She hasn't shut any part of herself off. Her ribs are exposed; her body is an altar, an antenna. She is participating in the kind of communication that is deep and soundless.

If you are creating from this energy pattern, what is at the front end is transformation—the shifting of things. Space and time are not legitimate barriers or obligations. You are creating to move mountains—to alter consciousness toward the mystic. You are interested in challenging the constructed ideas about what is possible and impossible. Impossibility is, in fact, a difficult thing for the Conjure Woman to buy into. If it were impossible, how could she imagine it? Wasn't walking on water supposed to be impossible? Isn't resurrection supposed to be impossible? Isn't levitation supposed to be impossible? Isn't sickness a thing that is supposed to be cured only by modern medicine?

The Conjure Woman is *possible*. She lives in possibility, in the transformative capacity. She does not feel bound by her body or what she is supposed to believe about her body. She does not feel bound by dogma or what she is supposed to buy into relative to dogma. For her, God is in the details. And those details are things she can manipulate and change. If the person occupying this space is out of balance in it, I imagine it can look like egomania. It can look like the misappropriation of power. It can look like sermonizing. She can make it so that there is no space for the person who is inclined toward a more traditional way of knowing to show up without scorn or ridicule.

Either way, the Conjure Woman asks that we exist in possibility. She certainly intends to dwell in that space.

Attributes

- Self-reliance
- Suspended belief
- Deep belief
- Connection
- Change agent
- Or egomania
- Zealotry
- Misplaced power

Exercise for the Conjure Woman

Oh lord, girl, you are a thunder-smack. A shift in atoms. You are so much magic it must be hard to be so connected. The world must seem a strange place with its rules and "thou shall nots." Write the witch's brew. A recipe for your special brand of juju. For example:

> You will need to go to the rock. Pour three and one-
> fourth cups of yourself into her. Stir slowly. A rock is a
> deliberate pulpit. She is thirsty for the wind in your body.
> When you are empty, go to the river. Swallow six gallons
> of her secrets. She is trying to tell you what you forgot
> you knew. . . .

I love the idea of the recipe poem. You can use it with anything. A recipe for loneliness. A recipe for disaster. A recipe for lasting love. But this poem is about the ingredients that make up your magic. Whatever that magic looks like to *you*. However it functions in your body, in your consciousness. Show the rest of us what it is constructed from. Show us how to get there. Be expansive in the telling. The spellworker's heart is a ritual. Give us a way to access it.

Examples of This Archetype

In the Congo, there is a widespread belief in child witches. The Western interpretation of this belief says the dire circumstances that plague Congolese people and trauma they have experienced are responsible for such a wild assertion. And yet the children themselves talk of flying in the night sky. Some were fed plates of cyanide and did not get sick or die. There are testimonies of militiamen describing a little girl flying above them. I have long held the position that while some of these narratives may be convoluted, at the core, the cultural context of the Congo makes not only the *belief* in witches possible, but it also makes witches themselves possible.

In this country, in the seventeenth century, there was an enslaved woman named Tituba. She was owned by Samuel Parris of Salem, Massachusetts. Tituba was one of the very first women accused of practicing witchcraft in the Salem witch trials—and she confessed to it.

In Central and West Africa, Mami Wata is a water deity. She inhabits individuals in her cult and "rides" their bodies for hours. There are men and women in the cult, but women are often the ones who are inhabited by Mami Wata, whose cult is an amalgam of Western, African, and Indian traditions. She is depicted as being beautiful, with unpredictable moods and a penchant for conjuring wealth for her practitioners and also cursing (with poverty or mental illness) those who anger her.

And lastly, in Gloria Naylor's book *Mama Day*, the character for whom the book is named, is a Conjure Woman. Mama Day works with the natural world. In the book Mama Day helps a woman who is having difficulty getting pregnant. She brings the woman, Bernice, to a house and positions the woman with her knees up. Mama Day then places a freshly laid egg from a chicken inside Bernice's womb, and when the moon is at a certain point in the sky, Mama Day breaks the shell of another egg and hands it to Bernice to eat. Bernice becomes pregnant shortly after.

Mama Day was the oldest daughter born to a seventh son of a seventh son. This is not a coincidental detail. The number seven is regarded (in many traditions and faith practices) as a number of some power and significance. In kabbalism, seven is the number of the natural world. Seven days a week. Seven notes on the musical scale. Seven directions: left, right, up, down, forward, back, and center. Nachmanides, also known as Rabbi Moses, a twelfth-century Jewish scholar in Spain, wrote a great deal about the weight of the number seven, should you be intrigued enough to wish for additional readings.

seven

The **Wombed** Woman

She ample, she big, she a wide, wide road.

Mama, women like you are impossible
There is no template for your kind of red-ribbon resilience
My daddy did not have the right circumference
To carry you, river woman, you
Are made of so much marrow
And he so indulgent in geography
The mud on his boots always
Looked like departure.

I wanted to love you as he should have
To reassemble your bones
Back into the flesh-borne masonry that
Looks the most like heaven
To genuflect under your apron
To swallow the psalms you pour into soup pots.

Mama . . . women like you are mostly mythological
Mountainesque matriarchs
Whose stories we borrow from
To keep some starch in our backs
Stars in our eyes . . .

Your resurrection songs lift the sky
Into my throat.

You were bone and tidal blood making biscuits
in the morning.
You are every yellowing page in my journal
You are everything I know about mothering.

I make up stories about the you I find
In the first few pages of that one old album
Every picture is frayed at the edge.
The wild in your eyes is a perch to fly from . . .
Without the spill of daughters oozing from the yawn
in your thighs . . .

Who were you before you split open?
Who were you before you were mine?
You are all I know of mothering . . .
And I am nothing like you, Mama . . .
You are all I know of mothering . . .

And I am nothing like you . . .

The Wombed Woman is the mother. The matriarch. The widest door. The best love. The first nourisher. The feminine template. We came into ourselves through her. She is the fruitful one. The fertile earth. The authority of women. Her body is authored by the construction of your bones. Releasing your body split her own in two. The severing, the otherworldly mathematics of one becoming two keeps residence in her muscle memory. Even if she is not the nurturing kind, her body never forgets what it offered. How it danced a death-birth ritual. How it bled. How it shook. How she lay down and became an earthquake.

I always planned to be a mother. My own mama was/is so expansive and heart conscious. I have known a mighty example. When I was a younger, I talked of having seven children. A great big busting-at-the-seams family sounded like a life. Children everywhere. My children. Folks I made from *myself.* I had a steady media diet that consisted of shows like *The Brady Bunch, Leave It to Beaver,* and the *Mary Tyler Moore Show,* and the mothers all made it look so soft, so easy. My own mother's composition is one that also suggested ease. I was almost an adult before I realized how much stretching she had done and was doing in order to parent me powerfully.

I had my first child at twenty-four. I was a grad student working on two master's degrees at the time. When I found out I was pregnant, I felt the atoms shift in my body. I had always been concerned mostly with myself. But there was *somebody else* occupying my body. I never felt so dangerous—dangerously female. I never knew I could love in so wild a way. But I was consumed by the wellspring of feeling that I was already carrying for what my belly was holding.

I'm thirty-nine now, mother to four children, and my capacity for nurturing sometimes surprises me. Three boys and one girl: I do not know how I *did* that. How did all of that alchemize from my body? How did I *do* that? What do I do with all that I carry for them? Every day they walk out of the door to enter the world, go to school, become magnificent others, it feels like my guts are exiting my body. Releasing is not an easy task for the mother. Even if it is a temporary release like letting them go to school, letting them go with friends, it's not easy. There is so much to protect. I have never been more acutely aware of how damaged and damaging the world is until I became a mother, a Wombed Woman.

When my first child was born, I had a C-section. Later that night I had the most spirit-busting nightmares I've ever had. I was driving on a long dark road with my newborn son strapped in his car seat in back. I could not see where I was going, but I was driving so fast. I was aware of my speed and made more afraid of how dark the road was because I was traveling at such a high speed. I did not slow down. My heart felt like it was going to snatch my chest open. I was so scared. Suddenly there was a speed bump, but it was a mountain of a speed bump. When I hit it, the car seat went flying out of the car and was swallowed up by the cavernous dark. I screamed myself awake and the emotional pain I felt was a razor blade. I wanted to die. I remember buzzing frenetically for the nurse, demanding that she bring me my baby. She was irritated and did not want to fetch him. I growled at her and got my way. My son came in swaddled and sleepy. I clutched him, squeezed him hard and cried. What would I do with a love like this? How would there ever be enough of me left what with all I felt for him? What would I do if anything happened to him? How could I know I was mothering him the right way? I knew I was nowhere near as patient or as gracious or as forgiving as *my* mother. I knew I had not learned her deft touch. But I also knew this new identity, mother, was a wide, wide mouth, and if I was not careful, I could be devoured—or worse, I could devour.

I didn't write much when my children were small. I was a poet, even then, but it was difficult to return to myself or anything that looked like the me that I was before I became the me that was a mother. Breastfeeding. I didn't know my body could generate so many options for itself, for others. Sleep deprivation. I *still* have not returned to a normal sleep pattern. After fourteen years, motherhood enacted acute awareness and an overdeveloped protective nature that meant I heard and hear *everything*. Deep sleep is not possible when I am on my post. I find myself fearful of things that were unremarkable to me prior to becoming a mother. Things like music. And television content. And how short miniskirts are these days. How many young black boys languish in prisons and group homes. How many young girls are violated, become pregnant.

I am a mother. How I parent is catalyzed mostly by fear and projection. That doesn't sound very enlightened, but it is honest. When I take the time to unpack what my views are with respect to being the Wombed Woman, I know that my rules, my boundaries, my guidance, and my lenience are all coming from either fear or projection. Rules are emergent consequences of fear. A curfew is less about the night and more about what I am scared can happen to them *at* night. How I present myself as their mother is about me projecting onto them what *I* think they need.

The Wombed Woman holds tremendous weight. She is the beginning of everything. Archetypically, she is always represented, always emergent. We assign roles like nurturer and comforter to her. And she is those things. But sometimes she is just the creator. Just the vessel. The means by which you got here. And in that I believe she *should* be honored, if for no other reason than your arrival. If the mother is not composed of much nurturing or comfort, it is a great and terrible source of pain. Her unwavering support and care is quintessential to our development. If she cannot produce it, what is left is a wound, an imbalance, a thing that can cripple us.

In my own experience, the women I know who did not get what they needed from their mothers have a hole in their chest. A big one that, at one time or another, was/is emotionally debilitating. It seems to have conditioned their experiences and relationships with other women. They often struggle to trust women, to feel connected to women, and I would posit that this is because the feminine template for them was one that suggested disloyalty, dysfunction, abandonment, cruelty. It's hard—very hard. What looms large about these same women for me, though, is that they are, themselves, amazing mothers, supernatural in their commitments to their children. I have seen them become cathedrals in their mothering. It is an act of worship, of deep-belly, all-encompassing, love. Their children are the beneficiaries of what they themselves did not receive. I don't know how they did it. But they did—they do—every day. Maybe they took that old hurt and let it be an opportunity, let it be a road map for where not to go.

If the Wombed Woman is out of balance, she can be a destroyer. Anything that can create can also bring doom. She can lord over her children in a way that does not affirm their right to be here. She can cause real destruction—destruction to the psyche, to the soul. My first real encounter with how destructive the out-of-balance Wombed

Woman can be came when I was in middle school. There are two big examples that jut out for me in memory. The first was my friend Jacisha's mother. Jacisha was in the world more than most girls I knew. Promiscuous and irreverent, she was a conflagration of black-girl flesh I had not been introduced to before. When I met her mother, Doris, I noticed the same pattern of behavior at work. When Doris spoke to Jacisha, she called her names. Bitch. Slut. Hussy. These were not terms she used in anger (not that that would have been a justification). These were terms she used regularly to address her daughter, and I thought, well, yes, no wonder Jacisha thinks so little of herself. She exists in a perpetual verbally abusive context that offers no daylight or room to imagine herself in a wider way. It jarred me. I had never seen that before. Jacisha died when she was fourteen, so I have no idea what kind of woman she would have become. What I do know is that she carried the wounding she received from her mother like a shroud.

The second example was right next door. There were twin girls who lived in the white and green house to the left of us. They lived with their uncle Tony. Tony was a young musician who smoked copious amounts of marijuana and stayed up late most nights trying to make a hit record in his basement. He seemed like a nice enough guy, but I couldn't understand why he was a more appropriate choice to parent than whoever their mother was, wherever she was. The girls were juniors in high school when I started interacting with them and being invited over. I soon learned that both of them hid terrible burns that covered the landscape of their bodies. One of the twins was significantly more maimed than the other. She always wore long-sleeved shirts and pants no matter the weather. When she felt comfortable enough with me, she changed her clothes in front of me one afternoon, and I saw the twisted gnarled flesh underneath. I must've been staring because she said, "My mama did it. She did it to my sister too. We were babies in the crib, and she poured boiling water on us." I did not know what to say. How could a mother do that? What kind of brokenness is that? She bore you. She held you in her body. How could she destroy what she created? I had no reference point for any of it, but I remember being so grateful for my own mother, who had always been gentle, who had never hurt me.

I still think about those girls sometimes. Last I heard, they are mothers now too. I wonder what they render to their children. I wonder if they stare at the scars they carry and envy their children's unmarked bodies. I hope their children have unmarked bodies. I hope that those girls have done something supernatural with their scars, that they have grown them into slogans about *never again*. I hope they know a mother is a thing that only *begins* with a birth ritual, but is made real in the work that follows. The soul work. The gardens you plant in your belly after delivery. What can become of your heart.

If the Wombed Woman is the energy pattern you most frequently occupy and are trying to create from, I imagine what's at the front end of it is guardianship—care and control. You make creation your business. And if you are in balance, you love what you have created because it came from you. You want to offer newness. Mothering and creativity can be and (in my view) should be a cross-pollinated affair. When I threw all I had into my babies and left nothing over for the writing, my sadness consumed me. I did not parent as effectively because suddenly the children were responsible for me not living out my gifts. And that is neither fair nor accurate. Your children are evidence of your bounty, your monsoon-like ability to make things manifest. So make things manifest. Even as I write this, my four year old is underfoot, asking for cereal and having long-winded conversations about action figures. I am indulging him, and I am indulging this. My mothering has gotten more creative as I have dug into my creative other life.

If you are out of balance in this energy pattern and are trying to create, what is at the front end could be neglect. Perhaps you feel neglected or have been neglecting yourself or others. Either way, you would be well served to find a way to leave it in your art as opposed to letting it take up residence in your body. When you create, you can regard it as an act of self-love, of bringing the nurturer into nurturing.

Attributes

- Comforter
- Nurturer
- Provider
- Creator
- Resourceful

Exercise for the Wombed Woman

You are the first need. The first connection. The one from whom life happens. This is an incredibly prodigious position. Write a poem that names the things you've "borrowed" from your mother. You can do this even if you did not have your mother; it just means that the lessons she gave you all happened by way of her absence. What did her presence or absence teach you that you use in your own mothering? What do you imagine she would tell you now? What advice would she give?

It can be purely from your imagination, or if you had the experience of your mother, name her legacy as it is attached to your own ideas about motherhood and/or womanhood. For example, "I take from my mama the exploding Crock-Pot with the collard greens peppering the ceiling. She taught how to keep my soup pots full. . . . I take from her the closed knuckled wailing that never makes it past the ribs. . . . I learned from her how wide women are. We know better than any how to grieve." Use stories from your experiences. Use images, snapshots, songs—anything attached to memories of your mother that illuminate how she influenced the way you show up in the world. Try for at least ten things—ten memories, ten stories, ten images that all provide you with ten lessons that you have fashioned into your ideas about the Wombed Woman.

If the things you are pulling from are negative or murky, don't be afraid to name them honestly. But while I am interested in you having clarity, I am not interested in you being overwhelmed. So look for the lightning rod in what you offer. Something powerful and important that you've extracted, even from the hard stuff. Especially from the hard stuff.

In the same vein, if your mother showed you goodness and you learned from it something harder, be authentic about *that*. A womb is a world, and sometimes, sometimes a world is a wound. But it is also an opening. Yes, an opportunity.

Examples of This Archetype

I am loathe to throw out examples for this energy pattern. The Wombed Woman is so many things, so many versions of creation—and destruction. It seems too obvious and convenient to invoke the usual examples of her. Yes, the Virgin Mary when her story is a creation story. Yes, Kali, when her capacity for destruction emerges.

But really, the mother is the alpha. I always thought it was interesting and inaccurate to assign that word to describe a masculine principle. The mother is the first in everything. There is nothing without her. Whether she is Joan Crawford or June Cleaver, she is still the hunt for how we got here. Etymologically, *mother* means "that which gives birth to something. That which is the origin or source of something." And *womb* literally means "any place or part that holds, envelopes, generates . . . or . . . to grow in secret." There is nothing in either word that predetermines what the mother *does* after birth. The birth itself is what defines mother. The growing of a thing. The originating principle of a thing. Period. Anything else we attach to it is the stuff of our own construction. "She did this, so surely she will do that," which, in any other context, is a flimsy and unreliable method of understanding anything, is, in fact, a flimsy and unreliable way of understanding the mother too. Perhaps, *especially* understanding the mother. My truth is that anything that can create is a hard thing to fit into a small space. The Wombed Woman is an origin; she is large, and she is complicated.

eight

The **Journey** Woman

Where you runnin' off to, girl? You leave before you enter.

A Letter from the Girl You Can't Keep

An entrance don't coo
Like an exit

It ain't a better ballroom
Than a highway, a dirt road . . .
Some far off unknown place

I keep hearin' the hills
Say: *come dance girl*
And my feet go lookin'
For them songs
What's the use in bein' still?
With so much world
To pirouette in

I wanna get it all over me
The soot and sparkle of
A thousand cities
A thousand late nights
In the heat of nowhere

My bones don't do
Nothin' for me
When I'm sittin' still

So I be runnin'
These feet to wildfire
Sashay shimmy stomp
And slide on down

I'm a Saturday night
Every mornin', baby
Pullin' up sunsets
I ain't seen

Don't look for me
To stay, baby . . .

I'm already gone . . .

The Journey Woman is ever moving. She is the quest-seeker. The traveler. The flight. The fancy. The door that is perpetually opening and closing. The exploring soul. She is looking for . . . something—herself primarily. Her individuality is wrapped up in the journey, is insistent on the journey, is *defined* by the journey. The world is a fine stage for the performance of self-discovery. A deepening of, a heightening of, her own understanding about *herself* is what catalyzes the Journey Woman when she is in balance and aware.

She fascinates me for a number of reasons. Hers is the adventurous spirit. Any epic tale is in possession of a protagonist who is bold in discovery. Granted, most of these protagonists are men, which is another matter for another book, but I have always been drawn to the idea of not needing to know what's ahead in order to forge ahead. To stick one's chin out over one's feet, to crane our necks into the unknown because there is a story there, one we can author, one in our own handwriting. It sounds so romantic and brave, so important.

So much of our constructed reality is what it is because someone elected the journey. I think about it in an African American context here again. Under an oppressive system, I think complacency is easier than movement. That's what makes oppression what it is. It is so stunting that it can convince you that the world is too much a howl to step into, that the world is peopled with brutes who will snatch at your soul at the first sign of independence. Best to stay close to whatever plantation you came from. Best to be a sharecropper for the man who's owned you since before you were born. At least you know what his cruelty looks like. Do you really want to risk exploration only to discover something that might kill you quicker?

It had to be paralyzing, the fear of striking out on your own, of seeking a new beginning. After slavery ended, a good many people stayed put. They remained close to the familiar. But others wrapped their bones around hundreds of miles elsewhere, maybe looking at the North Star trying to see what promises she would make, and headed into the unknown, seeking . . . seeking.

My own family's migration to Denver was about my grandfather's willingness to try on the journey and my grandmother's willingness to imagine that Little Rock, Arkansas, was not the only someplace that could hold her. These were important but fleeting moments for my grandparents, though. Those two beautiful people were the predictable, reliable, get-somewhere-and-sit-down kind. Being still has never brought me the same kind of contentment it brought my grandparents.

It costs something to be what you are. I imagine the Journey Woman knows this intimately. She is not constructed in stillness. She isn't the template for what a woman should be. She has seen that she should want the predictability of a spouse and children and respond with zeal and enthusiasm to the domestic tranquility found in a quaint house and white picket fence. And it is possible that she has acquired those things. It is, in fact, plausible that she has acquired at least some of those things. Women are conditioned to seek and then step into that reality and call it a life well lived. But for the Journey Woman, those things do not quiet her need to *move*. She may deny her need for a time, but it is always present in her, seeking an audience that only the world, and full access to it, can give. She may be the housewife in appearance, but if she is the Journey Woman, she is soaping the pots while imagining herself in some other far off place, doing something, anything, that is *out there*. If she does not permit herself to demonstrate her inclinations authentically, she probably negotiates great sadness—or anger. She wants to be in the world. She wants to know the world, as a means to know herself more fully.

Archetypically this energy pattern is recognized as appropriate, celebrated even, when men hold it. The seeker is Christopher Columbus, David Livingston, men who went "bravely" forward to "discover" and "explore." I hope I don't need to point out the irony in such examples being held up as models. They are also examples of what happens when the journey is so focused on the adventure and the *adventurer* that the consequence is a blood ritual, a pillaging, a claiming, a lack of regard for whatever is at the other end of the journey. Interesting that we still regard these examples as legitimate ones.

What is even more interesting to me is the way in which women are not permitted to feel a tugging at their own spirit that tells them to get up and go . . . somewhere. The woman who indulges that inclination is a woman in dereliction of her duty. Her duty is to home. Her internal compass that points her toward a journey is evidence of brokenness. A flaw in the design. She is not supposed to be positioned in the world that way.

I do not see the Journey Woman as flawed. In *Persuasion*, Jane Austen says, "I hate to hear you talk about all women as if they were fine ladies . . . none of us want to be in calm waters all our lives." The Journey Woman would likely say amen to that assertion. She is interested in a tempest experience as much as a valley experience. Because experience is what calls to her from within. Remember, she is seeking to investigate the matter of this world. She wants to hold it in her hands, examine its geography, toss herself into the middle, see what her spine is made of.

I connect easily with this energy pattern. I always feel eager to jump into the next thing. I rarely have a clear sense of what that thing is, but it is out there, and I am intrigued by it. I am electric and giddy when I allow my brain to imagine me trying on a whole new anything. It can be an occupational shift, a literal move, a trip wherein I am looking for a risk to take. I indulge a good bit of risk taking too. When I do not, I am mostly stopped by an internal critic that hisses things at me about being responsible and doing the "right thing."

I bludgeon myself for even having those urges. The conversations I have with myself about myself are scathing and accusatory. *Pull yourself together, Dominique. You have children who need you to be consistent and to provide them with a predictable life.* Some days I let that argument win. Other days my counterargument about living life authentically and passionately, and doing so as my truest self, is a bullhorn of a voice that I can't silence. And I don't want to. My commitments are ones I intend to honor. I do not see why a seeking nature is regarded as antithetical to that.

I suppose if the Journey Woman is out of balance with herself, if she is more a runaway than a seeker, it is problematic. This is the woman who does not know why she has to leave. The woman who cannot commit to things because she is afraid of being responsible. The woman who is too self-involved to recognize when the journey doesn't make sense. How does the explorer become the wanderer? Is that shift in consciousness an easy one to see clearly? Perhaps for the beholder it is, but for the Journey Woman, that might be a slippery slope. An explorer knows the mission. They know why they've set sail. They know the consequences of being boundless. They've grappled with it and accepted it. The wanderer is, in one way of thinking about it, directionless. They don't know where they are going. They may not even be clear on how they'll get there—or why they're going at all. They just know they wish to leave. But perhaps the wanderer is not directionless. Perhaps she believes that *every* direction is the right direction. She hasn't bought into the idea of needing a sure thing or a clear view in order to pack her bags and go.

On some level it must be hard to be relative to the Journey Woman. She always slips through the fingers. She is so perpetually wind-borne. Some of us want the people we love to be nearby and formulaic. When they are not, the relationship feels fragile. Never being able to predict what they might do or if they will stay challenges a traditional framework, and not everyone is interested in such challenges.

If this is the energy pattern you are creating from, what is at the front end of it is dissatisfaction. Life is calling you into it from elsewhere. And that could be purely because you know if there is a *here*, then there is a *there*. And you wish to know about it all. *Here* may feel like a cage, not a home. Or perhaps, it's not exactly that *here* is a cage, but *there* is an obligation you believe you have to yourself. So much art is made in the name of dissatisfaction. So much beauty is born out of the restless heart.

Attributes

- Adventurous
- Explorative
- Courageous
- Or restless
- Noncommittal
- Flighty

Exercise for the Journey Woman

The Journey Woman needs to pursue something. If she isn't, she is dissatisfied. As a creative soul, you can use the journey itself as your muse.

Because movement and experience is your thing, try writing ten post-cards. If ten feels too taxing, try for five. Each postcard is a place you would like to go, be it a real place with real geographical coordinates or a place in your imagination.

Each postcard should be written making full use of all five senses. Let us see the place with you. Let us feel it and hear it and touch and smell it with you. Show us the scenic route. Feel free to embellish.

After you've described the place, write down what you expect each place to offer you. What will it teach you? What will grow in you there? What challenges do you expect to come from each one? What disap-pointments? What joy? Do any of them feel like home, a place where you would actually stop and stay? For example: "This is the gray grit musty musical that is Philly. See the African street fair plump with won-derful? Everything sizzles here. Cinnamon and tobacco voodoo settles in the throat, rumbles, and does not move. . . . I could live here. Leave my bones to these concrete epistles. Can you see how delicious it is?"

Put yourself entirely in each place. You love the journey. Show us why you love it. Make us know it the way you know it, the way you wish to know it—*why* you wish to know it. Be deliberate about what you choose. Awareness is important. And by all means, use the exercise to travel, to move. You are the Journey Woman; it is given to you, to move.

Examples of This Archetype

It is easy to think of women like Amelia Earhart in conversations like these. Reading about her as a child, I remember wondering about what her journey-driven life cost her. If she ever regretted being so far flown. If her husband chastised her in private for being so literally "up in the air." I never forgot what she wrote to her husband in the last letter he received from her before her final journey. She said, "Please know I'm quite aware of the hazards. I want to do it because I want to do it. Women must try to do things, as men have tried. When they fail, their failures must be but a challenge to others." My favorite part, aside from the obvious feminist tinge, is the business of naming, so simply naming, what drove her. She wanted to fly planes because she wanted to fly planes. Period. She was not running away from her life; she was soaring into it.

nine

The **Shapeshifter** Woman

She a slight of hand. She a slippery sort.

I come into things dawn-dew slick
I make morning come to me . . .
Open my mouth and sing
You my teeth . . .
They are totems of stories
You're listening for.

Do you know what happens
When a woman becomes
An ache?

Everything is Sassoon in her.

To love her is to slip the
Wilderness under your tongue.
Catch the thorn-drunk sound
Of her shiftin' better than weather.

She can look like you like it, man.
Watch her look like you like it, man.

Watch her be an empty drawer in the kitchen.
Watch her be a breadbasket full to bursting.

Kaleidoscopic slick-handed changeling woman.

You can't know her
She too clever for that . . .

You can't know her
She too clever for that.

The Shapeshifter Woman is whirling. She is a master illusionist. She can spin your top. Her holograms look like real people. She always looks like real people. It's possible she is every one of them. It's possible she is none of them. What you see is not necessarily what you get. More to the point, what you see can shift radically to become another thing entirely. From my cultural tradition, shape-shifting is a powerful and deeply respected/feared attribute. In Navajo literature, the skin walkers were those who, upon adorning themselves with an animal pelt, could assume the body of that animal. The ability to wear your body like a sheet, to be able to become another thing, is fearsome and, in some contexts, problematic.

Archetypically, I suppose the Shapeshifter Woman could be regarded as the trickster, the wily, crafty character who brings confusion. But she is not so narrow. My consideration of the Shapeshifter Woman looks at her as wider than that, deeper than that, driven to change forms by experience, and by no means as a purely pejorative figure. Consider this: If the Shapeshifter Woman uses slight of hand or mischief as a way of being in the world, isn't it possible, probable even, that her presentation is borne out of self-preservation? We are all fundamentally trying to get our needs met.

In an African American context, shape-shifting was and *is* a cultural keystone. Being born into a societal construct that positions you as the "other" is dizzying—and damaging. Historically, Africans who endured a Middle Passage experience found themselves parceled out, renamed, stripped of their language, bought, sold, regarded as possessions, and made to work for the benefit of others. The hierarchy was clear, and it was oppressive. Some of us (in fact, I would posit *most of us*) became students of the game. We studied. We watched. We learned what our captors moved like, how they spoke, what they spoke about. We watched how they interacted with their families. We paid attention to where the fragility was. We learned what angered him, what behaviors incurred his wrath and brought down brutal consequences. We understood what *Massa* wanted. He wanted a crushed and conquered person. We knew he trusted the person who seemed to have accepted his fate best. The ability to appear to be what *Massa* wanted was an invaluable resource for enslaved African people. The slave who cooked in the big house, who nursed the children, who polished the silver, could also be *the spy.* She could make herself look like the obedient kind. She could smile and "yes ma'am" better than any. It was a hologram. One that let her gain access. One that gave her useful data about what *Massa* was doing and when he was leaving, and who he talked about selling off and who he planned to beat.

The Shapeshifter Woman, as she was constructed in that cultural context, was powerful, necessary, brave, and brilliant in her chameleon-like capacity. We needed her as a matter of surviving our experience. But if I move that analogy forward, not much has changed. I am the "other" almost everywhere I go. So many spaces I have occasion to occupy are acutely homogenous. In fact, they are often decidedly white, male environments. Obviously I jut out quite profoundly as a colored girl. My proficiency in the art of shape-shifting is what has kept me alive in these environments and institutions. To appear to be what they need to believe about me has been paramount to my survival. The nature of oppressive systems is to crush what that system has deemed to be most unlike *itself.* And as much as I dream a world that does not bristle when differences happen, when diversity announces itself, I am not naïve. I know where I am. I know what predispositional thoughts exist about me by virtue of demographics and other frivolous categories I am supposed to squelch myself into. I know. And as a wise student, I know how to exploit that kind of ignorance. I know what to do to tuck in when tucking in is the best strategy. And I know what to do to jut out when jutting out is the best practice.

This kind of espionage is almost a prerequisite (in my mind) for managing race, gender, and socio-economic politics—all categorical systems that ask for *my specific* identity to be tied to a kind of ritualized submission. When I am "the spy," I can make it look like I have adhered rather nicely to the role given to me. And all the while I am gathering information, fortifying myself, learning the pass codes, and then entering a space that is typically reserved for groups to which I do not belong, and the ruling group (for lack of a better phrase) is always surprised to see me. I'm being honest. If I am being *entirely* honest, most marginalized folks have developed this skill. Some more than others. Some have grown it into a complex science. Some have a life that needs them to shape-shift all the time. Others maintain and preserve spaces that allow them to show up as themselves, as they actually are. Even if this space is their living room, among family members who are equally tuckered out from a full day's work of looking like something other than themselves in order to keep the lights on.

The Shapeshifter Woman is the craftiest kind. She is aware of you. She knows what you want, and she knows just what net to cast out in your direction, to bring you into her—or to keep you *away* from her. She's so slick we don't like it much. One consequence of being relative to her is that you cannot put your money on who she actually is. If you are even aware that she *is* a shapeshifter, she has most likely dropped the ball somewhere. When she is functioning as her most strategic self, the beholder is not clued in to the atoms she's shifting in order to present herself as you see her. The Shapeshifter Woman controls whether or not you see her at all.

The trickster archetype is pervasively male. Mythology and folklore and legend and even cartoons demonstrate over and over again that this kind of intelligence is housed in a man's body. This doesn't surprise me that much. The nature of patriarchy would make it difficult to grapple with the idea of women having ulterior motives. Women who might actually be *pretending* to be in agreement with the power structure(s). Women who have capacity enough to be *pretenders* at all. It surprised slave owners that slaves were having secret meetings, learning how to read in spite of the laws against it, getting married without permission, and organizing revolts and disobeying. And that they were doing all of this while cooking the food and picking the cotton and tending the fields and washing the dishes—all of the trappings of the *obedient* sort. Oppressive systems always, *always* grossly misunderstand or fail to recognize the abilities of those they oppress. And that is how oppressive systems are infiltrated, that is how they are compromised, and in some cases, that is how they are brought down.

I've been having a lot of (read: too many) conversations about rape culture lately. Too many because rape is a consequence of a brutal and broken system of power. But women seem to want to talk about it as a problem men have. And I understand why that's the default. But a broken system of power needs our compliance to be what it is, to keep itself in practice. I say this all the time in the context of slavery, and every single time I say it, the room is fractured. But I will keep saying it. A system that survives on submission requires a group of people who are going to submit. If they do not submit, the system cannot be what it is. Slavery needed slaves. If you refused to be one, things fell apart.

In the case of gender politics and rape culture, I want to be clear: there is an acquiescence that has happened. It has been a slow brew. I remember the first time I heard the rap group 2 Live Crew. I remember the first time I heard a rapper by the name of Too Short. Their content was shocking to me. I didn't know men could speak about women that way and actually get to make CDs. The two aforementioned "artists" were regarded primarily as underground. They did not get played on the radio stations. You did not see them on TV. And then I remember when they *were* on the radio, when their videos *did* make it to television. That was a critical juncture. The culture (men *and* women, black *and* white) could have reviled their work and insisted on its swift removal. But that's not what happened. Acquiescence happened. Silence happened.

I also remember the first porn film I saw. And the second. And the third. There were things imbedded in those media forms that tried to convince me that women were things—things to be participated upon. That men were exercising a seemingly preordained natural right in dominating us, in calling us names, in relegating all that was good or valuable about us to quick quips about sex and cup size and the expediency of various vaginas. I remember being shocked first. Then mortified. By the time I was seeing it and hearing it pervasively, I had concluded in my own mind that that's just what men do. And our job was to survive it.

Women have done some wound-driven shape-shifting. We have pretended to not be afraid. We have pretended not to be offended. We have pretended not to be maimed. We have been in the company of men (and other women), and we have listened to our own bones crack under misogynistic language and politics. We have seen it and we have heard it and we have shape shifted into what looks like acceptance. Hell, some of us even laughed at the jokes wherein *we* were the punch lines. It is so much more convenient to be "one of the guys." But if the guys are out of balance, if the guys are operating from a violation imperative, then by our acquiescence, by our shape-shifting, we are making the lines between acceptable and unacceptable behaviors indiscernible.

It is such a difficult conversation to have. It is further difficult to be able to unequivocally know when the holograms we project are ones that by their very nature create an imbalance. What are the consequences of my pretending to be smaller than I am to play into the paradigm? Even when I am "the spy," what are the consequences? There have to be some. I am not naïve enough to imagine that just because my intentions are righteous ones, the resulting consequences are also righteous. The math is not that simple.

When the Shapeshifter Woman is out of balance with herself, she could look up one day and be unable to remember who she actually is. She has been spinning webs for so long, her own personhood may be compromised as a result. It can be a dizzying and, yes, dangerous practice. It is important to remember where home is. To be able to locate all of your parts—all of the things that tell you who you are. If you've been donning a disguise every day, I imagine that can become difficult.

I have talked principally about the Shapeshifter Woman as being motivated by a righteous cause, a survival strategy, but there is another model: The woman who is the masterful manipulator. The one who tricks you in order to take advantage of you in some way. The one who does not present her true self because her agenda is to take from you, to convince you of something that will set you up to be exploited. Now, I am still predisposed to believe that even that model is about getting a need met, but that doesn't make the practice any more right. I know what it's like to fall in love with a hologram, and to not recognize it as such until I am in shambles and my heart is broken. I know how unfair it feels. I know the chagrin that lives hard in the body when you realize you've been duped. The pain it inspires is the heaviest kind. I have not personally experienced, nor have I been guilty of, the kind of shape-shifting that is designed to hurt someone. When I have felt it, the shapeshifter was trying make herself an acceptable suitor, a worthy candidate for my affections. She was, in essence, trying to *keep* me. The hurt is still the hurt, however.

Manipulation requires acute intelligence. Manipulating shapeshifters have to know something about you in order to manipulate you. They have to play on your personality, your experiences, your wounding, and your position. If they haven't bothered to learn these things, they don't have enough data from which to construct the hologram you are most likely to believe or be moved by. My most jarring experience of this came in the form of a rescuer. This person not only recognized where my fragility was, but she also set up a string of events that would throw me into chaos. And when I was appropriately disheveled and in need, she then swooped down and dressed herself as the proverbial knight in shining armor. She was saving me from the things she herself had created in order to position herself in my life. By the time I realized what happened, and how deep the rabbit hole actually was, I was devastated and emotionally limp.

The Shapeshifter Woman in balance is the Jedi. Out of balance she is a manipulator. Either way, she is keeping her true self at least partially hidden. She is composed of many, many selves. She is trying to get her needs met. If she is pulling from the murkier aspects of that reality, she is willing to do so at the cost of great suffering or confusion for others. If she is pulling from a higher aspect, she is managing all of those faces with a "do no harm" clause underneath.

To create from this energy pattern is to be the chameleon. What is at the front end of it is duality. It is quite possibly (and much to my chagrin) the slam poet who reads a gut-wrenching work about molestation because she sees she has five female judges and thinks such a topic will wrangle them emotionally in just the right way. The reality is, she has neither experienced nor been particularly moved by the subject matter. She is writing and reading what she thinks will help her be successful—and it may not be who she is or how she moves in the world at all. I have been a participant in many a rigorous conversation with other poets about this dynamic. The appropriation of feeling and perception that is so prevalent in the world of competitive poetry. It makes me uncomfortable. I do not like being manipulated. Still, every artist who is trying to be published, or printed, or hung in a gallery, has thought about their audience and tried to produce something they think the audience wants. I don't have a problem with that in and of itself. Where I struggle is when the artist is giving the audience what they want and that thing is not a real representation of the artist. But in the interest of consistency, perhaps that artist is employing that tactic to position himself or herself to be able to do the art that *is* a true representation of who they are and what moves them. Perhaps the tactic is about getting a foot in the door. It still makes me uncomfortable, but if we were talking about a woman or a person of color doing the same thing to crack the corporate glass ceiling, I wouldn't even be mad. So my contradictions are sadly apparent.

I have a lot of empathy and space for the Shapeshifter Woman. At the same time, the creative process, writing specifically, for me is about being myself. Unpacked and unfiltered and unaltered. It is the place where I get to tell the truth about myself. The hologram business is not a solicited thing in the writing for me. It should also be said that the Shapeshifter Woman might be motivated by deconstruction. She could be responding to the hierarchy of subjugation and oppression by assembling herself as the spy.

Attributes

- Intelligent
- Socially aware
- Deliberate
- Costumed
- Or tricky
- Manipulative

Exercise for the Shapeshifter Woman

This does not need to be a poem. Instead, I am interested in you writing in free form about what payoff you get from changing forms the way you do. Talk about how you know what face to put on. Where you learned it. The benefits to you, personally and/or professionally. Talk about the people who do not get to see you as you are and why. What's at risk for them knowing? Then talk about the people who *do* get to see you as you actually are, and why they have that access. If you cannot name anyone who you've granted full access to, explore that. Where do you go or what do you do to show up as yourself? Or are you always the changeling? If the latter, try to identify what that costs you. Are the payoffs more expansive than the consequences? Who is helped by your act? Who is hurt? What would the world need to look like in order for you to take the costumes off? What would need to change? What people? What systems? What rules? Try to empty out here. If you are struggling to identify the people and/or things that keep you from a true representation of yourself, then it is quite possible that your shape-shifting is entirely driven by you. And if there is no need for it, nothing at risk for you showing your true form, is it a practice that you need to keep?

Examples of This Archetype

In terms of the canon, *she* is a *he* for the most part. Some Native American people have a figure called the Deer Woman who is a shapeshifter. She is a woman who can become a doe. And the doe, depending on what indigenous tradition you're referencing, can be responsible for matrimony or be the punisher for wrongdoings.

In many Afro-Caribbean spiritual traditions, there is a belief in the Orishas. The Orishas originate from continental Africa and found their way throughout the New World via the trans-Atlantic slave trade. Orishas are essentially spirits that reflect the various manifestations of God and the ancestors. Eshu, sometimes referred to Ellegbara or Papa Legba, is the Orisha I was divined to represent. Dualistic in nature, Eshu is the trickster. He is reflected in folklore as Brer Rabbit, the cunning character who used his wits to outthink those in power and to bend social mores as he saw fit. He was later adapted for Disney in a motion picture called *Song of the South*. It is said that Eshu causes "tribulation that leads to maturation and finally inspiration." The architect of confusion in order to usher in awareness, Eshu is a shapeshifter. He can look like an old man or a young man, a man or a woman. He changes his form depending on the circumstance and the beholder. He changes his form depending on what is needed.

In the Urban Dictionary, one of the definitions of *shapeshifter* is "[a] female that appears initially to be attractive, but when seen from different angles looks to be ugly or mediocre. This pattern can continue and makes it difficult for males to know if the girl is really attractive or not. Shapeshifters are often good at hiding their ugliness with hair, certain makeup, or clothing in very specific instances." The term is then used in a sentence: "I can't figure this girl out. The first time I saw her, she looked really hot. Then on our next date, she looked totally average. She's a shapeshifter."

Whoever put that definition together should know: the Shapeshifter Woman is working with more skill sets than what her makeup bag is composed of. Remember that. She is the transformer. The transmogrifier. The woman whose left hand looks right. The woman who can make Monday morning look like Saturday night. She is the mimicking one. She can outwit and outmatch. Her guise is purposeful and deliberate. And don't you forget it.

ten

The **Warrior** Woman

She an open mouth. And an open mouth got teeth.

She gon come for you
Mister, in your well-lit life
She gon come for you hungry
Seekin' the sound of your flesh

She gon come for you

Warrior woman
Embattled woman
Strategy woman

She gon come for you

Bled out back broke bayin' at the moon woman
She gon come for you
Til you see her
Til you hear your own bones clutchin'

She gon come for you

A rhythmic dread
A rusty blade
An unsheathed soul
Yeah she gon come for you, Mister . . .

She hungry
She hungry
She hungry

The Warrior Woman is a strategist. She is positioned on rooftops, the watchful one. She is a sharpened, seasoned blade. She is acquainted with the night. She has called her own blood forth. She knows precisely how it moves in her. She is the untrembling hand, the gospel of bone marrow and steel. She is the samurai. The firm one. The unwavering one. The one who is poised. The one who is ready. She never questions whether justice and truth are profitable or dangerous. Hers is a whole-body experience—an unfaltering one. And her whole life is about meaning it.

The Warrior Woman knows how to kill what needs killing. This can be as literal or as metaphorical as it needs to be. She knows how to get rid of what needs to go, how to come to terms with it, how to put things behind her. She is not catalyzed by resentment or even extreme anger. She does not let angst or loathing create a jingle in her bones or a flick of her sword. In fact, she knows resentment and loathing promote weakness. And weakness is something she can't afford.

A warrior is not a thug. She's not a gangster. She's not a woman who happened upon a weapon. She is not a soldier, because soldiers follow orders. They do not get to make decisions about what battles they fight or with whom; that authority rests with their superior officer and the system into which they have inducted their bodies. No, the Warrior Woman is chieftain. She is autonomous and stretched deeply into her individuality, her capacity to fight, and to do so her way.

She is constantly measuring out what kind of opponent she can be. What kind of opponent she already is. What kind of strength she is possessing. She is not trying to grow this strength in blood. She is philosophical in commanding her bones to go looking for the entrails—entrails that are not physiological but psychological. The Warrior Woman goes inside to argue with her own soul. She reasons that if instinct tells us to run from a gunfight, she can retrain her own brain to run toward it. To be unafraid of the hail of bullets. She tells her eyes to see past them. She tells her body to be a tuning fork. She is a conscious, painstaking warrior, and her antenna is high. She doesn't need nor does she go looking for allies. If you can challenge the spirit, if you can test the flesh, if you can fight alone, well, you can fight.

Warriorship is an inward journey. She is looking hard at her fear. Whatever would destroy her, such as fear, is something she puts her hands to at once. Whether by circumstance, habit, or discipline, the elusive and scarcely noticed tremor in a warrior is rerouted to something sturdier. She is not training merely to overtake an enemy. She is training to run directly into a worthy adversary, the righteous fight. Her ideals are fixed firmly about her. Once she knows what stirs her to action, she will not retreat until she has spent herself. She is not flailing wildly. She is not spitting in the wind. She is focused, and sure, and knowing. She is the willful dance of overmuscled consciousness. And it is an often-solitary dance. The pathos of the Warrior Woman is a vast study of her own nature.

My own understanding of this energy pattern tells me that the warrior makes her peace with loss. She is attuned to the fight and its potential consequences. When I think about the Vietnam War, what comes up for me in that particular conversation with history was how formidable an opponent the Vietcong were. How they watched and waited. How they studied and surveyed and hid. How they reasoned that they would fight and fight no matter the bodies. That they would sacrifice their own bodies. That they were willing to lose everything so long as America did not win. You cannot easily defeat the person who is not afraid of losing and losing big. American *soldiers* went into Vietnam and faced *warriors*. The difference proves the fight.

For a woman, this is a great big bit of business to step into: to repackage self-preservation into something that involves not the asking for help or supplication to this or that. To let her will manifest itself into something with teeth. To react as little as possible but to instead go inside and prune the tender parts of her nature. To grow blades where petals used to be. Even the woman who is not necessarily sentimental or soft has to wrestle down certain instincts. To repel all that which would drop down on her uncertainty or hesitance.

The self-discipline is awe-inspiring. I imagine her on a mountaintop. Going there is a willful act of social disengagement in order to fully and bravely engage the *self*. How do you know what your insides look like until you take yourself away from what is familiar, what is comfortable, what is predictable? She will sit and she will grapple and she will wait. When she comes down from that mountain, she will not wish to be anything other than what she is. She will have watched her own fears topple over. She will know the ledge, and it will not frighten her.

The Warrior Woman is the persistent kind. She is fiercely loyal—to her own ideals and to those who uphold those ideals, to her kindred. She is Spartanlike. Her strength has coordinates she has plotted carefully. She is not looking for a fight. She is not even eager for one. In fact, I would posit that the Warrior Woman wants a peaceful existence more than most. She does not have a casual relationship to violence. The person who knows what their capacity for violence is, is a person who has seen it in practice. Everything else is theoretical at best. She has seen how flimsy flesh can be, and how resilient. She knows what a blade does, what a bullet does. She has heard the labored breathing of a person who is trying to exit their body. She knows how the lungs sound when pushing for oxygen that does not come. She is not squeamish. She is clinical.

If the Warrior Woman is out of balance, she is arbitrarily barbaric. She is a biting woman. She is an unmanaged anger. She is rancor and upset. All she knows is her venom, and she is amenable to spewing it out all over everybody. There is a great hurt in her. She has made anger her religion. She is likely unreasonable and always ready to access her contempt. In fact, if she is out of balance, the world itself may feel like a contemptible place. Everywhere she looks, people are doing it *wrong*—whatever it is. Everywhere she goes, she is shrouded in ill feeling and discontent. I would posit that the Warrior Woman who is out of balance with herself is nursing a wound that produced real sadness for her. Somewhere along the line, that sadness got rewritten into anger. Anger does feel more powerful than sadness sometimes. Whatever or whoever the architect of her original wound is, she has made sweeping promises to herself to never feel that kind of hurt again, to never allow for the same kind of vulnerability. The problem here should be apparent.

Warriors pick their battles. They know when to fight and what weapons they will use. They know what the damage will be. They've considered it, weighed it out before pressing on. When that is out of balance, there is no strategy to the fight at all. Nor is there any clarity. Everybody is an enemy when the Warrior Woman is out of balance. She may be so entrenched in her anger that, if asked, she would struggle to locate what is driving it. The story she has made up about her rancor is that it will protect her from what might harm her. But she lacks discernment, so she imagines that everyone is poised to hurt her. She assumes the worst, about everyone and everything.

This kind of unchecked anger maims. And it doesn't just maim the guilty. It maims the innocent. It maims the woman who is carrying it. It is the corrosive kind, the cancerous kind. It sits hard in the belly and leaves the bearer unfit for most relationships. Not many are willing to stand near a person who is thrashing blindly. Even if she loves you, if the out-of-balance Warrior Woman has clipped you more than once. She has said unforgivable things. She has lashed out. She has accused. She has let herself become a weapon of mass destruction, and the safety is never on. She doesn't even know where the safety is. Your subsequent hurt may mean something to her episodically, but it does not talk her off the cliff in any permanent way. To do that she will have to go looking for what is driving all that rage. And most likely it is old and has nothing to do with the people who keep getting cut.

I know what this is like. My grandmother was a wounded warrior. I would say grief was at the bottom of the wound, but what was always at the top was rancor. She was stern and cold and not moved by how she might hurt you. She said things to me that shrunk my bones. She seemed to me to always be angry, and I never could figure out why. She had a loving and incredibly nurturing husband. She had students who valued her. She had a daughter who was composed mostly of sunlight. And yet she was red—a lot. I often tiptoed around her. I never felt like I was safe from an eruption. It was like living at the base of an active volcano. One way or another, the stuff in her belly would fall down around you like lava. As a child, I was stunned and silenced by it. As an adult, with deep pockets of my own anger, I roared against it. Arguments between her and me were seismic and awful. My grandfather always put his body in front of it and tried to keep the room intact. I carry a lot of guilt around for putting him through that. And at the same time, if faced with the same kind of bile, I react with teeth of my own—still.

I know how to fight. And not in the abstract either. I *know* how to fight. I know what knuckles feel like against my flesh. I know what it feels like to be physically attacked—and overwhelmed. I know, too, what I grew in myself on the other side of those moments. I know what I willed myself to become in order to keep myself safe. I know the warrior's heart. I have not been afraid to confront it—in myself or anyone else. Once you have reckoned with the slings and arrows, all that is left is endurance. Endurance and the clarity that comes from reckoning with what fight you have in you.

Some people do not wish to know this part. I would say my mother would rather remain aloof on the subject. She is not one to become too acquainted with blood and bone. I am composed differently. Sometimes I think it is a thing I need to fix in myself. Other times I know it saved my life on more than one occasion and wish to keep it—keep it close, honor it, give it a proper name. One of my sons is also a warrior. He is twelve, and so he doesn't know why he is fighting. But he is resilient and will not back down no matter the odds. When he is an adult and knows the world with a wider lens, I hope he is more strategist than battering ram. I hope he knows how not to spend his flesh on frivolous things. I hope he knows that the consequences of unmanaged anger are difficult to heal from. I hope he knows the warriors are ones who have engaged their guts, their internal universe, that they are philosophers, deep thinkers, heavy with self and personhood.

If the Warrior Woman is the energy pattern you are creating from, what is at the front end of it, if you are in balance, is discipline and control. Creation for you is the bramble moving out of the way. You have thought about and aimed at a target. You are not whimsical or frivolous in it. You come to the canvas because your art is the battlefield itself. The place where you come to test your flesh and examine your insides. Or perhaps your art is the reward at the *end* of battle. What you do with it, what you create, tells you if you've won or lost, if you fought the good fight, if your strategy bore itself out. Sometimes what our consciousness is nudging us toward requires a proper blade. It is possible that you create to unsheathe your sword, to examine your bloody knuckles and teeth.

If the out-of-balance Warrior Woman is trying to create, rage is at the front end of her creation. The art might assist her in exiting some of that anger. Or it might feed it, make it grow larger, more pronounced. She may be creating in order to stand and accuse, or she may be trying to find what quiet, what balm she can. The canvas for the Warrior Woman who is out of balance might, in fact, be where she dumps the bodies.

Attributes

- Sagacity
- Strength
- Deliberation
- Strategist
- Or angry
- Violence
- Cruelty

Exercise for the Warrior Woman

The Warrior Woman is master to her backbone. She knows how to fight because she knows who she is. This exercise can be done with a split screen. In other words, fold the paper in half or create two columns. On the left, write down all of the things you would go to battle for or against. These things can be people, ideas, systems, circumstances—whatever you carry that you interpret as a worthy adversary. On the other side of the page, or in the next column, list out all of the weapons you need to use to fight that fight. These weapons can be literal or more imaginative—that is up to you. I would encourage you to try and incorporate it all.

When you are done, look at your list and identify the biggest battle among them. The one that looms the largest for you. Perhaps the one that generates the most anger. Keep in mind this battle could very well be with yourself. Next, pick out a weapon from the list you created that you think would help you win the fight.

Once you have that, write a poem about this "enemy." How long have you two been at odds? Have you ever defeated it before? Is it the dragon that refuses to be slain? Describe your weapon fully. Describe the battlefield. What day the battle will ensue. How you will ready yourself for the skirmish.

It can look like this: "I bring to the fight, my teeth. They leave my mouth open. An open mouth is a good ally. It shows me how to scream, how to howl and pluck fear from behind my throat. I fight the stories I made up about myself. The ones that told me to be silent. The ones that locked every door. I have made my heart a flat green star. I will fight there . . ." Or a more literal languaging: "Brian, you are long gone, but there are bones between us. I am not content to keep them clanging in my closet, so I bring you out to face me. I am not so small now. You are not so large. I keep a hatchet tucked into a lace pillowcase. The handle is wooden, worn to splinter. I touch it and bloody my hands. This kind of fight insists on my insides coming out . . . getting all over everything. Know this. My blood is mine. I offer it at my discretion. As for yours, I will author its experience from the edge of the blade. . . ."

Be a strategist. Take an aerial view of the battlefields you've chosen for yourself. Make sure you are properly armed and defended. And by all means, be ready.

Examples of This Archetype

Well, the histography of African woman warriors is expansive. The Amazon women are probably most recognized. From early Greek accounts, they came out of North Africa—Libya, principally. These women were fearsome in battle and depicted as being large and ferocious. The Dahomey Amazons were an elite group of women warriors whose skills in the area of hand-to-hand combat commanded the respect of the French. In Ghana, an Ashanti queen named Yaa Asantewaa fought against British colonial rule. In Nigeria, Igbo women led an insurrection against the colonial government's attempt to exercise a tax on women. It became known as the War of the Women in 1929. In Liberia, women like Leymah Gbowee put their bodies in front of militiamen who were burning homes, forcing children to become soldiers, and using rape as a weapon of war. Leymah faced them down and did not retreat. Gbowee is responsible for helping to bring an end to the Second Liberian War in 2003. Her stand ushered in a period of peace and enabled a free election in 2005, which saw a new government run entirely by women, from the police chiefs to the president.

And certainly, let's not forget women like Joan of Arc, who commanded an army at the age of seventeen, who led France to victory more than once before she was captured and burned at the stake. And Zenobia of Syria, whose leadership defeated the Roman army. Despite the prevailing representations of women, we have a long history of relating to ourselves as fierce.

eleven

The **Third Eye** Woman

She sees it. She sees it. She sees it.

I can't tell you how I knows it.

Seem like lightnin' strikes on the inside
And I go tremblin'.

Seem like I can't stop the stories

They slide down
They slip in

I can't shake 'em no how
It ain't no regular dream
It ain't no picture stuck in the frame
It ain't no song you know the words to

It a old thing
It a new thing
It a thing comin' on

Comin' on
Comin' on

Sometimes I shuts me eyes to it
But the third one stays open
Keeps on seein'
What I didn't mean to know

Keeps on bringin' in the
Stories I ain't wrote
They push my eyeballs loose
Like gawd playin' marbles
In my skull

I say *be still* and *turn me loose*
But they keeps a hurricane shook
In the eye I can't close . . .

Wonder will it work when I'm dead . . .
Wonder will it work when I'm dead . . .

The Third Eye Woman is the seer. The knower. She comes into things by intuition, by instinct. She is the receiver. She is the bridge. The one most whispered to. She cannot but hear the voices. She cannot but know their names. She is the one whose spirit is old. What she knows comes into her, formless. It is a languageless land. It catches her at the ankles and pulls her under. She cannot help but be a door. She has always been a door, and it is always open.

It is difficult to have sight—insight, foresight, even hindsight is inconvenient clarity. We seem to take more comfort in leaving things to chance, or faith, or happenstance, or circumstance. Fate, the belief in it and the way some apply it, is a faraway notion with a script not written in our handwriting. If we do not know what is coming, or what is going, that is, for some of us, a more comfortable existence than one that tells us what tomorrow will bring.

So much of our existence, from my perspective, is about coaxing the brain into a kind of mediocrity. We are taught into numbness, a disconnected state of being. I attribute so many ills of the world to this kind of functioning. The Third Eye Woman is in a state of *wakefulness*.

The polarity between now and was or now and will be is a gap she does not obligate herself to. She can't really. In fact, I'm sure it would be convenient for her to be able to, but she is *open,* conscious, and thusly seeing. I imagine that for the Third Eye Woman, being stretches farther than thinking.

For me, education and social conditioning produced a kind of divorce between my conscious life and my unconscious life. They had been on speaking terms. When I was a child, they knew each other well. They talked to each other. They alerted me to things. And then private school happened and neighborhood violence happened and puberty happened and the misapplication of puberty happened, and my media diet became glutinous and my lens got decidedly narrow. Before I knew it, my intuition was a dead thing in me. She didn't stay buried, fortunately, but for a while she was gone.

The Third Eye Woman is in the universe. And that universe is her body and all of its facets. Further still, her existence is one that is deeply aware that the universe—the great big, everything, everywhere universe—is interested in *her.* Is moving with her. Is grounding her. Is all of her. She is acutely aware, in fact, that she has transcended the narrow confines and representations of the mind. She is not bound by it. This is important to unpacking who the Third Eye Woman is and how she shows up in the world. Because the mind is not reality. The mind is a simulated and constructed version of it. It is constantly interpolating, interpreting, categorizing, managing, packaging, reasoning, illustrating—on and on. But truth is not moved by what you think about it. What is true is true or real whether you can get your head around it or not. You can elect to ignore it, pretend it does not exist, close your eyes and your consciousness to it, but it goes on in spite of your mechanisms. It is undisturbed. The Third Eye Woman is not living in her head, despite whatever understanding exists about the seer's ability to see. If she was bound to her head, she could not see anything. Those kinds of polarities between body and mind are prohibitive in any conversation about clarity and sight. No, she is aligned in a way that permits an opening. In my tradition, this way of seeing is generally regarded as ancestral logic. Whatever and whomever preceded her is still available to her. Whatever and whomever are after her or ahead of her are available to her.

There are conversations about precognition, premonition, and presentiment that you may find instructive, but these are not dwelling places for this book. What I will speak to is the notion of linear representations of time and space. They have always proved problematic for me. My own understanding of the world and the *worlds* does not permit so narrow a study. If something *was,* then it is. If something is going to be, then it already *is.* Viewing time as some marching on, never looking back or forward thing always gave me pause. How is it confined to some tidy one-directional line? The universe is so big and possible; how can time be so simple? How can life be?

It seems to me that the Third Eye Woman is not the forgetful kind. Perceiving yesterday as gone seems to me to be willful forgetfulness. It is not about hanging on to yesterday or what was so much as it is about being mindful of those things and allowing them to still be a part of you in a living, conscious way. When people transition out of their bodies, the interpretation that they are now *gone* to us is also a kind of forgetfulness; in my mind, one we are conditioned to. It is a thing that is absolutely taught. In other countries, other cultures, other societies, there is a different understanding, one that permits a more cyclical or circular consideration. Time is unending and not subject to simple compartmentalism. Life is unending and not subject to simple compartmentalism. This way of knowing is derived from remembering. For me, it feels like self-remembering. Training your eyes to not just record what is on the outside in an easily observable way, but also what is on the outside in a less observable way. And then further to train your eyes inward, to see how many rooms you can get and keep open in the universe that is your own body.

Training your eyes inward is the difference between saying, "It is. They are. I am," and instead *feeling,* "It is. They are. I am." Feeling it from the inside. Feeling it until it stops being a recording in your head and is instead the stuff of your lungs, your heart, your blood, your bones. From there, the brook becomes a river, and that river an ocean.

It is not easy stepping into this kind of awareness. The linear is quieter. Forgetfulness is more convenient. The Third Eye Woman knows what is coming. She knows it like she knows herself. Precognition: The Third Eye Woman can *feel* what is ahead. She can feel it moving through her. Sometimes the feelings fall soft like downy flake. Other times there is a clattering in her. The trembling or roaring kind. She can feel the weight of what is coming. Presentiment.

When I lived down south, the town seemed to be brimming with Third Eye women. I was in graduate school at the University of Arkansas. The road I lived on descended into an uncarved patch of earth, a small forest just two doors down. Monticello, Arkansas, is an old place. It hasn't changed much since Reconstruction, I am told, and when you live there, that is not so difficult a notion to believe.

Right next door to me was a family of four. The father was gone most of the time. The wife looked like a wrung-out dishcloth, tired and sagging from the perpetual heat. The youngest girl was prepubescent and unremarkable. The oldest daughter, who looked to be in her late twenties, was mostly catatonic. Sitting in front of a window that looked out onto their front yard, she just sat and swayed. Mrs. Vernell, the woman across the street, was the first person who told me that the older daughter had been possessed. She said the house the family lived in used to be a storefront church that had been damaged by two separate fires before the preacher up and moved to another space that was not so subject to scorching. The family was given permission to move in after their own house caught fire. Men came and snatched the cross down off the top of the building, and they moved in. It was shortly after their arrival, Mrs. Vernell said, that the oldest daughter became possessed. She told me that she dreamed it the night before. Said she saw the girl, who she described as having once been quite talkative and lively, floating over the house with blood in her mouth. She said she woke up and tried to shake the image, but the image was inside her. When she went back to sleep, she dreamed of the daughter again, this time with pupil-less eyes, breathing a fog over the house. The next day, the mother came running out of the house screaming and asking Jesus to protect her. She howled and carried on about her daughter being "ridden by the devil," and Mrs. Vernell sat on her porch watching the whole thing, knowing.

I listened to this story with some cynicism at first, but that only lasted a minute. By the time she was done with the story, I *felt* what happened more than I heard it. When I asked around (and I was pretty fastidious about asking around), I heard the same description of pos-session from so many people that I let go of doubt. I suppose someone could argue here that it was a kind of communal hysteria. Fine.

Mrs. Vernell also knew when her husband would die. And he died—quite unexpectedly died. She knew I was pregnant with a son before I knew I was pregnant at all. She knew I would get four A's and one C that first semester, and I did. I never shared anything about who I was with her, but she could always see it anyway. And it always seemed to pain her in some way.

Miss K was another Third Eye Woman. She saw two white horses moving in a syncopated way down the road. It took her a second to record the fact that there were no perfectly white horses around, certainly not two matching ones, and even if there had been, they could not be moving together in so coordinated a way. Miss K watched them as far as she could. When one horse looked left, the other did as well. They turned the corner and were gone. The empty road then produced a clear and present image of Miss K's brother. She remembered how he loved horses. She was trying to process what she was seeing when something came into her, and she knew her brother was going to die. She told me about the dream the next day, and she told it in a very resigned and stoic way. I was lost in fascination about the two horses and was trying to imagine what she was describing, and the whole time she was grappling with the loss of her brother—a loss that had *not* happened yet to a person who was healthy and entirely able-bodied. I tried to tell her that the two horses did not have to be some premonition at all. I tried to tell her that she was reading the wrong things into it. I told her to call her brother and confirm that he was fine, and she did. And he was. They chatted for a little while, and when she hung up, she cried. She was grieving for him, and he was not dead. It created some real dissonance for me. Until he was killed two days later. After that, any resistance or doubt in me left and was replaced with humility.

My own mother can tune in to a frequency she is not supposed to be able to hear. She has dreamed things and felt things and known things, and they were all spot on in terms of what was going on with me. And in most cases she did so from hundreds of miles away, when I was in college and she was in a PhD program. I never questioned how she did it. I always chalked it up to our connection, but I am sure it needs a broader conversation.

The Third Eye Woman is an emphasis on transtemporal awareness. She may be born with it, or it may emerge in her circumstantially. She can see way outside herself. She can see way into herself. She may not even be able to access all of that high-powered insight when it pertains to her own life, but she has a high frequency and it is a part of her experience. It has already been said, but it bears repeating: the Third Eye Woman is a doorway, and it is open. She sees things as they actually are or will be. In Biblical language she would be a prophet. She is the oracled one.

If you are creating from this archetype, what is at the front end is vision. Your waking life can assist you in being a visionary. It is a place to bring the conscious and the unconscious together. It certainly has been that for me in terms of my art. I sit down to write without an agenda or an idea. I sit down to write because something in me is tugging at me and wants an audience. Often times when that first line comes, I have no idea what it means. The lines that follow are my attempts to understand that first line. I experience it as my unconscious life trying to become a part of my conscious life. And sometimes my unconscious life includes borrowed memories and experiences.

Sometimes the language is not mine. Sometimes my unconscious life is a movie reel, and I haven't met any of the characters before, but they know *me,* and they are insistent on a dance. The creation process is buoyed by the visionary. The envelope is always stretching. The boundaries are required to go away. Visionaries make the art that can change our lives, shift our paradigms, and show us what we did not know to be possible. The visionary sees much. And they see it in a different way. Art becomes the best kind of hallelujah when it is being generated from a person who is positioned in the world this way.

I have certain poems that came from . . . somewhere else. These poems have different weight and vibration than ones more informed by my deliberate consciousness. I am glad I make space for them. I am increased every time. Most artists, in my view, are poised to allow for their mediums to become a powerful *medium.* If they are open to that.

If the Third Eye Woman were out of balance, I would posit what is on the front end probably looks like self-doubt: *Who am I to have all this data?* It is difficult to come to terms with. She may feel incredibly challenged by her gift. She may also run into those who cannot celebrate her gift, and that creates dissonance and wounding. She may be entirely resistant to the sight she has. It may frighten her or generate concern for her. The Third Eye Woman who is out of balance may also be withdrawn and intentionally removed from larger society in an attempt to manage her experience. Someone with that many rooms open in her consciousness will need strategies for how best to carry it.

Attributes

- Vision
- Open
- Connected
- Sight
- Or self-doubt

Exercise for the Third Eye Woman

Because sight comes into the seer, because it is given to her, take a moment and write about what insight, what foresight, what precognitive moment you've had or experienced. What did that feel like to have that kind of vision? Did you doubt it when it came to you? Did you turn away from the information, or did you lean into it? Did you tell anybody, or did you keep it to yourself? Why did you respond the way you did? If you felt fear, name the fear. If you felt anger, name the anger. Or confusion or exhilaration—name it all. Did you wish for blissful ignorance, or did the information save you or someone else from hardship?

When you have written it all down, write a note to your consciousness. Tell her where you want her to be keen. For example, "To the part of myself with the most vision, stay ever vigilant about the children. Whatever I should see, let me see. Whatever I should know, let me know. Let me be omniscient there. Do not let my adoration blind me. Do not let my assumptions keep me from knowing what is most true." You can train yourself into consciousness. You can ask for what you want. Do it. A third eye is a heavy, though important, resource.

Examples of This Archetype

I am going to offer only one here—the one that I think about most often. September 1963, in Birmingham, Alabama, a man planted a bundle of dynamite at the Sixteenth Street Baptist Church before service commenced. Choir practice was in full swing upstairs, and children were in the basement, readying themselves for Sunday school. A woman whose children attended that church had a dream the night before. She saw blood pouring out of the church. When she woke up, the dream had frightened her so that she told her children they could not go to church that morning. They protested and resisted until they saw how upset their mother was, and they let go of their protestations and stayed, resentfully, home. When the bomb went off and the family felt the aftershock from their own living room, they wept and thought about their mother's dream from a very different place.

I do not know what that woman touched in her consciousness that gave her that kind of foresight, but whatever it was, it saved her children that day. There were other children who were not near as lucky. There were clergymen digging through the rubble, finding small limbs. There were children trapped beneath the debris. And there were four little girls who were obliterated that day. Insight, foresight, precognition, whatever language you wish to attach to it, is a powerful and sometimes life-saving, life-altering gift.

twelve

The **Howling** Woman

She got a hole in her chest. She keep her fist in it.

Howling Woman

She is a pocketbook with the seams
Pulled out.

Been clutterin' up her
Womb with men
Who ain't got no Jesus at all.

Just howlin' her
Saturdays from under her skirt

Plucks the tender kisses
Their hot mouths could not make
From her babies
And listens for rain clouds.

Howling woman in the moon-stretched night
Like a steeple in a valley of rotten fruit
She keep pullin' the weather
Out from the hem of her skirts

She remembers when she was cathedral.
How her hips didn't hold

No rent parties inside 'em
How she knew what she sounded like as herself

How the last man took up too much space in her body.
Slid out of her without a smile ·
And she couldn't find God nowhere in the room.
Just a howl.
Just a tremor.
Where her body used to be.

The Howling Woman is a dirge. A funeral procession that may or may not have a body. She is a lamentation. A sorrow-walloped soul. Her grief is an empire. A landing place. The only house she stays in overnight. She is the bluest hour. The anonymous groan. She is an agony. She is an agony. She is an agony. She is the bottom, the very bottom, of grief.

Grief is a character. It can be an unrelenting one. It can be the biggest thing in the room. It can be the only thing in the room. Grief has a shape, a sound, an urgency. It does not wait until we are ready. It does not wipe its feet before entering. It does not knock on the door or ask for permission. Grief is a tyrant. It is heavy-handed and unapologetic. It can drown out the perfect, euphonious melody of your life.

The Howling Woman *lives* in sadness and grief. She is consumed by it. She is bleary-eyed and grasping because of it. It is dogged work for the Howling Woman to keep her head above its current. Her grief is unabridged. Its grip is insistent. So much of who she could be or would be is floundering underneath the weight of the sadness she holds. If she only could be like Atlas. If she only could get out from under it. If she only could find some daylight. If she only could know it was hers all along.

Grief is an old French word. Its literal meaning is "to make heavy. To be weighty and burdensome." How grief lives in the body is consistent with the etymology of the word. I have known grief to be a noose around the neck. It can be a most persistent emotion—more persistent than joy for some. *Depression* is the catchword for this kind of relationship with grief or sadness. And I think the language is right. Because to depress a thing is to take the air from it, to bear down upon it. Whoever is relative to the experience of depression is flattened and laid low as a result.

In many respects I feel like I inherited grief. It operates in my body like borrowed memory, as if it is encoded in my genes. There is a legacy of trauma and grief in the African American community. The same could be said about Native American realities, from whence I also came. So many bodies. The histography of suffering and cruelty, the legacy of slavery and massacres and genocide, the auction blocks, the plantations and reservations that were holding pens and slaughterhouses—all of it crowding in on the consciousness of a culture.

I think about the unspeakable acts committed against family members whose legacy is a present and right-now thing for me. It is the context into which I was born. It is not far away or in the abstract. My grandfather, who was integral to my development and actively parented me along with my grandmother and my mother, came out of the Jim Crow South. Born in 1911 in Little Rock, Arkansas, he grew up in such a shell-shocked post-Reconstruction reality, replete with mob rule. His grandmother, called Danny, was a slave. She lived well into his adulthood. Growing up in such a repressed/oppressed environment, and being reared by folks who lived through horror, cannot help but instill a kind of post-traumatic-stress-informed perspective and legacy. Add to that the lack of emotional integrity and/or emotional literacy that was almost mandatory for my predecessors' survival. There was no way for my grandparents or their parents to authentically demonstrate the chagrin they must have felt, or the anger, or the horror that came from their lived experiences. To do so would have been risky. Better to swallow each bitter pill without wincing. To bleed internally if you have to bleed, and to not cry out when it hurts. That kind of dissonance is mind warping. I grew up with people who never shouted, never cussed, and never shook their fists, never roared. Not even my grandmother, who had the most teeth. Even when she clipped you, it was rather quiet—biting and stinging, but quiet.

But *all* of them cried. All of them held deep river sadness in their bellies. All of them mourned—something, someone. I felt the sadness almost more than I saw it acted out. I could feel it when my grandfather's heart was heavy. I could see it in my grandmother before she said anything. I always feel my mother's low-rumbling grief, which she keeps mostly to herself.

I know how to be sad. I know it really, really well. I have known it since I was a little girl. My childhood was a practicing of it. I have very few memories whereby I wasn't holding some kind of lament. Sometimes it was a small and easily patched up thing. Other times it was a monsoon, a hurricane. It washed over me. It took things with it. It left me fragile and quaking. It left me uncertain and disassembled.

In my adult life, I have tried to be intentional about having a different relationship with sadness and grief. I don't deny it if it comes online, but I don't let it run roughshod either. There are times for me still when I just feel it. There is no catalyzing event. No episode or interaction that I can look at and declare the culprit. Sometimes it just shows up in my body, and I feel it. I feel it all the way through. I try to locate the *why* of it. I try to be investigatory about it. Sometimes I can track it down and sometimes I can't. Some of the sadness feels old. Like it doesn't really belong to me. Like it's not really mine. It's a borrowed sadness, a bequeathed one. I don't know if I have language enough to explain that fully, but it's real for me. It feels ancestral. It is guttural and deep and bubbling over in a place I can neither touch nor name. It can be the consuming kind. I have, on more than one occasion, been devoured by it.

When I was in college, the sadness was acute. I was struggling with so much about myself and my experiences. I was away from home and thus felt displaced and ill equipped to deal with any of it in a way that honored me. So I was self-sabotaging and steeped in the loneliest kind of grief. I thought about suicide a lot. And then felt shame around that, and that shame only deepened my sadness. I eventually saw a therapist just so I had a place where I could empty out and say things out loud. And weep. And weep. After a while, there was enough room on my chest for me to be able to breathe. After a while, it didn't hurt so bad. After an even longer time, it barely hurt at all.

I can still carry some of that old, borrowed sadness from time to time, but when it shows up, I know how to save myself. Mostly it comes from my inclination to be satisfied. Sounds sophomoric, but it's true. I really like being able to belly laugh and frolic. I *need* to do those things so sadness does not get to have dominion with me. She visits, but she cannot stay. I do not permit that.

For the Howling Woman, this is not so simple a task. She is buried alive in her sadness. Something has driven her insides out. Something has festered and spoiled. She has a hole in her chest. She cannot (or maybe *will* not) stitch it closed. Her life is *defined* by her sadness. And depression is tyranny. It clangs and knocks. It feels like bloodletting. It feels like rotting from the inside. It is insidious in its ability to snatch at what could be peace. The Howling Woman's sadness is so seismic it intrudes on everything—her relationships, her interactions, her productivity, her clarity, everything. Depression fuels so many other subcategories of dysfunction. It is often what is at the root of eating disorders, suicidal thoughts, self-neglect, self-indulgence, addiction, certain patterns of abuse, hoarding, on and on and on. And once you engage it, once you offer it a seat at the table, it is loathe to leave.

I have known so many women who operate from this energy pattern. So many. Too many to even remember. What I know is that sadness hangs on. And what's worse, sadness can become a thing that you become dependent upon. The Howling Woman has made an identity out of sadness. She has convinced herself that her hurt tells her who she is. Her pain is as important to her as her name, where she grew up, what schools she attended, who she first loved, what she knows most. It is an onerous inconvenience to have this kind of relationship to sadness. It doesn't let much daylight in. It doesn't let many people in. And if they do get in, they are hard pressed to stay. Having a commitment to sadness is the worst of it. If you are interested in joy, then you are aware that your sadness is problematic. But if you are not convinced of your right to joy, then sadness is a familiar space to flail in. It may even feel safe. It may feel like home. The Howling Woman has inducted sadness into her bones. And for her, it feels almost impossible to excavate it.

Sadness does have its place. I believe entirely in the idea of emotional literacy and emotional integrity. Being able to access *all* of your feelings is, in my estimation, being a whole person. Living too entirely in one emotion or being unable to locate and connect with one, for me, feels like an imbalance. So by all means, sadness has its place. When my grandparents died, my sadness was acute. It was a reasonable response to losing two people whose impact on me is immeasurable. But I did not stay there. I did not make it a home.

If you are trying to create from this energy pattern, what is at the front end of it is obviously heartbreak, melancholy. You may be using your art as a way to bring your sadness into the room for others to see. Part of your torment may lie in believing that people don't know what you are going through or what you carry. Your art then becomes a testimonial to your internal bleeding.

Or you may be using your art to try to escape your grief. You may be trying to make a world, one composed of beauty, music, sunrise, possibility. You may be trying to right (write) the wrongs. Because sadness is so present, you may be creating work that others call lifesaving. You may find that people are in awe of your truth-telling and transparency. They will tell you they know what you mean, or they have been through something similar. I find that people are so grateful to hear your grief stories, how you grapple, how desperate you became, how you managed to erect yourself despite whatever was tearing at you. But mostly, people are listening for how you *survived* it, how you transcended it. If you are the Howling Woman, you may not yet have a transcendent story, but you can use your creativity to devise an escape route. Some of the most important and prominent artists of our time did just that.

The Howling Woman needs to come to terms with the understanding that her happiness need not be so anemic. She is caught under the rubble. Instead of digging her way out, instead of issuing a distress signal, she is trying to hang curtains in a house that has been demolished. She should know the only way to get out is to *leave*.

Attributes

- Melancholy
- Heartsick
- Troubled
- Sorrowful

Exercises for the Howling Woman

You are carrying a wound. It has been allowed to hiss and lie too long. For the first exercise, try to describe your sadness. Is it a black and overmuscled steam that comes into the room and knocks you over? Is it a fire you can't put out? Is it a rainstorm? Is it a dark room with a low ceiling? Is it a cellar you are trapped in? Is it a tornado? Is it more personified than that? Is it a person who told you things that made you question your worth? Is it a faceless figure who stands in the doorway and calls your name or beckons you to come closer? Describe it fully, the sadness. Be as detailed as possible. Whatever you say should be instructive for you because it gives insight into how you are relating to it.

Next, have a conversation with the sadness. Tell it what it should know about you. Ask it questions, if that feels right. Perhaps you want to know how it got there or how long it plans to stay. Accuse it of things. Perhaps you need to speak to it in anger. Perhaps you need to speak to it with comforting, consoling language. Write it all down. This is not necessarily a poem. For me, it is an opportunity to engage sadness in a powerful and intentional way.

It is also incredibly important for you to acknowledge in this exercise that you and your sadness are not the same. You and your sadness are not inextricable from each other. It is its own thing. It is occupying space in your life, but it is *not* your life.

The next exercise for the Howling Woman is to write down all of the things that generate sadness for you. All of it—people, events, losses—all of it. Write it all down. Fill up as many pieces of paper as you need to until you have emptied out.

Once you have done this, on a separate piece of paper, write down all of the things that give you joy, that bring you peace, that make you feel happy, hopeful. Write down all of the things, events, and people that help you know the full expanse of your royal capabilities.

Once you have done this, I want you to take the piece of paper that holds the list of all the things that make you sad, and I want you to set it on fire. Watch it burn to cinder. Observe how quickly it goes once you decide to take a match to it. Sit with that experience for as long as you need to. And when you're ready, take the piece of paper that holds the list of the things that give you joy and fold it in a small square. Put that square inside of a flowerpot and cover it with soil. Plant something there. Something that blooms beautiful. Something that flowers and stretches and invokes the sun. Let your joy list have the same opportunity to flower and grow fruitfully. Leave your howling in the flames, woman, and be the phoenix. Be. Be.

Examples of This Archetype

Famous jazz singer Billie Holiday always struck me as a Howling Woman. She was without the consistent presence of her mother for the first ten years of her life because of the kind of migratory work her mama had to do. When she was eleven, she was raped by a neighbor. When she was twelve, she was an errand-runner for a brothel. By the time she was thirteen, she *and* her mother were working as prostitutes at a brothel in Harlem, and when she was fourteen, she went to prison for the crime.

Billie knew incredible success in her adult life once her musical talent was discovered, and in a very short amount of time she made a good deal of money making music, recording albums, and performing all over the country. But her sadness and wounding trailed her, and she began abusing drugs and alcohol. She went through prison and rehabilitation as a result of her struggles with addiction and was perpetually involved in relationships with abusive men. Grief was everlasting for her. A thing, it seemed, she genuinely struggled to move through. She died at the age of forty-four, and though she so impacted and reinvented American jazz, she could not find a way out of her own suffering.

I think about this woman all the time. It's not her music that keeps her in my consciousness. It's her sorrow and how it consumed her. Her wounds—her old, old wounds that kept her from knowing how big she could be. I lament that. I lament how much she must've cried alone. How often she felt pain. How that pain tricked her into thinking it was the biggest part of who she was. When I *do* reference her music, the sorrow behind the lilting bell-tinkle voice is audible.

thirteen

The **Violated** Woman

Somebody took it. Somebody took it. Somebody took it.

I ain't never met a woman
Who didn't look like a crime scene.

We so broken and entered

We so every day robbed

We so always snatched

We so always took

I don't dream of love no more.
It's a made-up suffocated story.
It keeps a blade in its back.
It's gon always bleed and
Turn to brine.

Naw, I don't go in for love no more.

A man who don't turn your flesh
To cautionary tape . . .

Is a man who ain't been born.

The Violated Woman has been mishandled. She has heard the sound of her flesh breaking. She has writhed under the weight of another. Her mouth has borne a fist. She has been a shudder. She has been a scream. Hers is the worst kind of story. Her hips pushed to shards. Her hands left knuckled and broken. She has been the scorned one. The torn one. The she-asked-for-it one. The one who grew barbed wire around her thighs. The one who fights to remember her body when it was not treated as a liability. The one who bled the sky with her prayers. The one who has been face down. The one who has been knees up. The one who has been a crime scene. The interrogated one. The dishonored one.

And the one who is most familiar to me.

Mine is a soul-snatching truth. I do not have many memories or experiences that belie the position that the Violated Woman is a predominate figure. Even canonically she is the most represented. The literature that is most celebrated, most often taught, is replete with her. The Bible itself bears this out. Book after book describes strife and pillaging whereby the women were taken, appropriated, and languaged as the spoils of war. Over and over again we see the Violated Woman as the *template* for what womanness means. Over and over. We are written as ruined women who, by virtue of biology and cruel power-based systems, are seemingly obligated to grow a vast carrying capacity for institutionalized, ritualized, and systemic perpetual violation. The impact of that kind of epistemological violence and misogyny gets written into the consciousness of a culture and becomes an imperative. In other words, if the Violated Woman is the most recognizable representation of woman, then men are positioned to mishandle and misappropriate women, and women are positioned to be violated. And society will absorb it and normalize it in a kind of culturalized brutality agreement.

The Violated Woman has been bloodied by a certain psychology, one that has intruded on ideas about what it means to be woman. What it means to have power. And what it means to be born into a hierarchical framework that insists that womanness be regarded as synonymous with victim. I know how vitriolic I sound. And I don't care. Not now. Not anymore. The bile in my belly comes from so many exhausting years of scrapping for an understanding of womanhood that did not come with a rape clause. When I was in elementary school, I *knew* men took things from women and girls that they had not been given permission for, that they had no rights to. I did not happen upon some scholarly article. I did not overhear it in a conversation had by adults. I *knew* it. I knew it intimately. And it changed everything about how I saw myself, my family, my community, men, and women. The paradigm shift was swift, and it was severe. By the time I was in middle school, my familiarity with pedophiles was mind numbing. It was difficult to locate myself.

My best friend came from blue-collar factory workers who were very young parents. They had become pregnant with my friend at the age of fifteen and married at the age of sixteen. If I had to count the number of times I saw and/or heard my friend's mother being pulled apart by her husband, I wouldn't be able to do it, it was so frequent. I saw him punch her teeth out and choke her until her legs kicked out from under her and she was on the floor with his boot heel in her face. I saw him slap and snatch and throw her to the floor. All the time. Too many times. And I was twelve years old when I scrubbed her wounds out after he had raped her on a night when I was staying over. I know what her face looked like bleeding from every orifice. I remember how pink the water got. I remember her trembling lip that had a deep gash in it. I remember her broken tooth. I remember how she managed to weep in silence so as not to awaken her daughters. I remember how my knees shook and how I gnashed my own teeth and wanted a different body, one that did not come with so many slings and arrows. I remember asking whoever was listening for her to pick up and *leave* him—to run anywhere that did not require so much bleeding out. And I was spun into silence and a bottomless sadness and helplessness when, at twelve years old, I had the thought that no such place existed if you were a girl or a woman.

The Violated Woman as the template. What a dysfunctional world we live in if that is practiced out as a true statement. It is not a conversation I venture into much. Just to generate the language for it leaves me feeling war-whipped, battered, traumatized, and resentful. But I have sons. And the thought that they might elect to try on the power privilege written for them keeps me up some nights. They are so intact and unavailable to so much of this. But even in their naïveté there is an implied awareness of the hierarchy. They have known it since before they had language. Hell, I would posit that we *all* have. In that hierarchy they know that they are supposed to be somewhere at the top. And if there is a top, then there are folks being crushed on the bottom. And in this conversation, those are women folk. It is no great mystery then why rape and sexual violence statistics have such big and bloody numbers. It is no mystery why the relationship between sex and violence is so interconnected. Because by way of our cultural context, the Violated Woman is supposed to be *every* woman.

Of all the women friends I have had in my lifetime, only two do not have a violation story. Two—out of close to twenty. After a while I stopped regarding it as remarkable or noteworthy when yet another woman I became relative to told me about a daddy, uncle, brother, neighbor, boyfriend, stranger who had abused her and taken something precious from her without consent to do so. Because it was so pervasive it was *unremarkable* to me. And there's the rub. Once it is old hat, once it is a familiar perpetual occurrence, once it fails to produce the appropriate reaction in you, it has, for all intents and purposes, become part of our cultural identity. It is a thing that has been allowed to exist for so long, it's not an aberration. It is an agreement.

The Violated Woman has had her flesh held out for gawking. For appropriation. For misapplication. For usury. She does not even know if she believes in her own wholeness anymore. No one else seems to. The *inevitability* of her violation is embedded in the prevailing politics, media, and language of the culture she has membership in. If she cries out or calls for recompense or justice, she is regarded as vindictive and spiteful. Suddenly her protestations make *her* suspect. And that is the kind of sex and violence imperative that tears everything asunder—everything.

She is the one set up for destruction. She is the one who is supposed to feel it most profoundly and to carry it with a closed mouth and an abiding acceptance. Violation is supposed to be her *fate*. If it does not happen, well, then *she* is the lucky one. She is the one who exists in a minority, a strange group of women folk who have somehow managed to avoid the lash. The unraped ones, the unkilled ones, the unabused ones—they are the aberrations. The rest—the rest have felt the full weight of their womanness in the precise nature in which it was prescribed for them. It is an awful ugly. A deafening ugly. A soul-altering ugly.

When I read about cases that actually make it to trial, I expect to hear conversations about what the Violated Woman was wearing and how many sexual partners she's had. I expect to hear about whether or not she had been drinking that night and whether or not what happened to her was actually an unwelcome act. I expect to hear these things. And what's worse, I have learned my conditioning so well, I catch myself sometimes listening to the attack in her character and wonder about the authenticity of her accusation. That's when I know I have learned the lie the way I was supposed to. Because any woman who claims she was violated is operating outside of the code of conduct permitted her and to do that calls her into question, right? The dysfunction is paralyzing.

The business of scorning and shaming the Violated Woman is big business. Men and women both participate in the mechanism. Acquaintance rape is where I see it happen most frequently, but I would posit it's a general practice. The only time I don't see it is when the Violated Woman is not a woman at all. When she is a child, there is no shaming. Pedophiles are unequal in our eyes and in the eyes of the justice system. But if the Violated Woman is an adult, then she cannot be raped. At best it was rough sex, and she, feeling vindictive and shame-filled, decided to frame or otherwise tarnish the reputation of a man who had done no wrong to her.

When the culture has accepted rape as an inevitability, when the Violated Woman is the template for womanness, then the Violated Woman does not have real access to her own healing. Her body holds the memory that is maiming her, and society insists on her stoic acceptance, her silence, her acquiescence. My friend's mama never divorced her husband. She never ran away and sought shelter elsewhere. She never pressed charges. And no, it is most assuredly *not* because she enjoyed what was happening to her. It is because leaving is regarded as a dereliction of duty. The Violated Woman may believe that this is our lot in life, the only real birthright if you are born female: To bear the abuses. To absorb them. To play the part.

It sounds unreasonable and illogical, but it is, in fact, a thing that is built into what we are conditioned to believe about womanhood. I vacillate between crippling anger and sadness when I grapple with this. I do not like grappling with it. I am depleted from it. But I am deeply concerned with dismantling any paradigm that suggests my victimization is preordained, that my biology is, in fact, a liability.

What does the Violated Woman do with her experiences? What does she tell herself about her body? What does she tell herself about her abuser? There are as many responses as there are women, but I would posit that the Violated Woman, as I have known her, as I have *been* her, is entombed in her own body. If the body is where you live, then the Violated Woman lives in a ransacked home. The walls have been pulled down. The floorboards are torn up, bare and splintered. All of her prettiest things are gone or damaged. And the doer comes back to the scene with every new interaction the Violated Woman tries to have, every new relationship; he peers into the windows and jeers. The neighbors suck their teeth when they pass by the mess. They resent her for how devalued a piece of property she is. The police tell her she should have been more cautious. With a house that size, she should have thought better than to leave her windows open or to hang such pretty curtains. She should have known somebody would see it and want what's inside. Why didn't she install a security system? Why didn't she invest in padlocks? Why is she making so much trouble for the robber? How many houseguests has she had in the past month? Does she really expect anyone to believe her house was robbed when so many others have been invited in?

And the doer just jeers and smiles from the window. She sees him and believes she can never be whole, never be safe. She starts to condemn herself for hanging such pretty curtains. She believes she was wrong for having the windows open. She looks around at the mess that is left and believes it is her fault. She believes it *was* an inevitability. Starts to contemplate setting fire to the whole damn thing. Hates every room because they remind her of what was taken. Keeps the window shades drawn tight. Gets rid of the elaborate curtains that inspired the robbery to begin with. Sometimes she feels her loneliness and wants to invite people over. But every time she does, the doer comes back and stares at her from the window. She is uncomfortable in her own home, and it is a house she cannot break the lease on—not without losing everything altogether. So she sits in the dark, amidst the mess, and wishes she had a way to live somewhere else. Somewhere clean and unsullied. Somewhere with the walls still intact. Somewhere she could hang up pictures and leave the windows open without the inevitability of burglary.

The Violated Woman is evidence of a crime. Of war. Of maltreatment. Of violence: Perpetual violence. Sexual violence. Systematic violence. Linguistic violence. Political violence. Cultural violence. Media violence. She is not supposed to survive with her soul intact. She is not supposed to survive with her body intact. And if she has really learned the rules of engagement as it relates to patriarchy and oppression, then she will not only be violated, but she will also cleave herself to her violator. This is a difficult and tricky subject that triggers men and women alike. It's like Stockholm syndrome. At some level, any oppressed person wishes to know what it feels like to be on the other side. The other side looks so privileged and fortunate. They do not seem to be at the mercy of anyone. They are on top, and there is oppressed envy. They know how crushing and bruising the bottom can be. It's the old adage "if you can't beat them, join them" at work. And we are all participants in that strategy for the sake of survival. But it costs us something. Something significant. Something real. Something that pulls us further and further away from our purpose, our capacity.

I will say it again. The Violated Woman is a wound—a cavernous one. It is physical, psychological, emotional, and social. She may have come to believe that she is supposed to operate from a broken place, from a fractured and damaged place. She looks around, and so much about her lived experiences and the prevailing messages support this idea. If she is trying to create from this place, it is possible that what is at the front end of it is distrust. Her art may read like a diary entry. It may read like an open letter to the destroyer. It may read like an arrest warrant. She may be creating to believe something different about the world—something different about herself. It may be hard for her to imagine that she can be handled warmly, but something in her feels riotous about that. Something in her knows it is unjust and unequal. She wants to get her body back. She wants to get her heart back into her chest. She wants to know that what happened to her matters—to somebody. She wants to occupy her skin with intention and joy. She wants to release the muscle memory that binds her. She wants the wind on her back, the sun on her face. She wants to feel her spine straighten and her voice return. She wants restorative action. She is tired from carrying herself like a broken thing. She wants a reckoning. She wants it to stop. She wants it to stop. She wants it to stop.

Attributes

- Wounded
- Angry
- Distrustful
- Pensive

- Fragile
- Voiceless

Exercises for the Violated Woman

For the first exercise, I want you to write a poem/letter to your body—to every part of you. Each line begins with ownership. For example, "This is *my* mouth. She is not for closing or stuffing with syllables shrunken in silence. She is *mine*. She has always been mine. I will use her to the hilt, to the very last breath of me. She and I will practice roaring. I will forgive her for the sizzle and spill of unsaid things . . ." Speak to every part of you.

This is reclamation business. It's not light work. Reassemble all the parts. Fashion them into something mighty. Be a sculptor. Make it as beautiful as you are—and you *are* beautiful. Make it—and *you*—necessary.

For the next exercise, I want you to go back to the scene of the crime. First get yourself grounded; you will need that to move into this place. Then go back to where you hurt. Go back this time with an aerial view. Go back this time in full possession of all your limbs. Go and write a different story. Write the story of your escape. Write about how you got away. Write about how you fought back and won. Write about how this time when you called out for help, people showed up in droves. Write about how you kept your blood to yourself. Write about how the destroyer did not win. Write the destroyer out of the story. Write them as small. Write them as regretful. Whatever you need to happen can happen. Write it down. Make a new chapter out of that other one.

Remember, you are not who you were. There are things you know about yourself that you did not know then. Use them. Gather up your resources. Trust that they are many. Trust that you are safe. Write it that way. Write yourself safe. Write yourself whole. Go back and fetch the woman you were before something happened to you. Attach wings to her. Stitch a song in her throat. Let her be fleet-footed. Let her spine be straight. Let her heart be available for a big, big love. Let her win.

Examples of This Archetype

There is no shortage of examples here, in the literary world and the literal world. I think about the character Mayella Ewell in the classic novel *To Kill a Mockingbird.* I think about her a lot. Because she was the pivotal figure who falsely accused a black man, Tom Robinson, of raping her. The focus on Mayella is usually on the accusation she made as a way to discuss racism in this country. And that is a fair and accurate depiction.

But that is not the only conversation about Mayella. No, Mayella Ewell was a young woman being abused by her father. She existed in mind-numbing poverty. She was forced to care for several younger siblings who wore her to the bone day in and day out. She had, what seemed to be, a rather loveless existence. She was worked half to death and lived in a house with a man who would beat her. The bruises she attributed to Tom Robinson in actuality came from her own father. She is a character I have both loathed and found real empathy for. She was seeking affection and kindness. She took a liking to a black man (Tom Robinson) who passed by her house daily on his way home, and she attempted to seduce him. When her father came home and saw her trying to kiss Tom, he flew into a rage, beat her, and then forced her to falsely accuse Tom of a crime he himself had committed. She is tragic. And she is familiar.

I think also of the character Bone, the young girl in Dorothy Allison's book *Bastard Out of Carolina.* Bone was repeatedly beaten and pulped by her stepfather, who finally escalates and rapes Bone in her aunt's home. Bone's violations were so severe and so perpetual, reading the book felt like I was maiming myself. And yet Bone too is familiar. She is so many girls I grew up with, so many women I am friends with. She is the lead in so many stories. The names change; the violations are the same. But the hope is too. The hope is still available in these stories. The hope for reclamation and hope for the kind of strength that is just on the other side of survival. Yes, that too.

fourteen

The **Beggar** Woman

She a need. She say, "Mista, spare a dime."

You don't need to know why I need it . . .

Why my hands be stingily sweaty
Glazed in empty
Seekin' somethin' that
Might could feel like rain
If I shut my eyes tight enough
If I keep my eyes hungry
Maybe you'll give me a ride someplace
I just wanna get out in it
Go where you go
Sleep in a bed that greets me like
A warm wide mouth

You don't need to know why I need it . . .

You just need to hand it over
I'm standin' here lookin' at you, ain't I?
With my face pulled under from
Too much wind . . .
Ain't I lookin' you in the eye when I ask for it?
Don't that mean nothin' to you, man?

You don't need to know why I need it . . .

But I been climbin' my own life
With my knees bled out
I been needin' so long
Seem like my need get
More grit
Seem like it want more for me than I do . . .
Seem like I can't help but
Figure you got it mister
Witcha pretty four car garage feet
Just gimme somethin' . . .
Gimme somethin' . . .

You don't need to know why . . .

Just gimme somethin'
Til I know what *enough* feels like . . .

The Beggar Woman has her hand out. She is sure she needs something. She is sure she doesn't have it or know how to get it on her own. Her life has not satiated her. She is uninvolved in some higher form of self-reliance. That, for her, still looks like asking someone else for what she needs. She has not been taught to build it herself. She does not want to build it herself. Her want is the galloping kind. Her need makes her seem embryonic. If it's hot, bring her a cool towel. If it's cold, put a sweater around her shoulders. If it is lunchtime, make her something to eat. If it is bedtime, tuck her in and dim the lights. She is unlearned in the art of independence. It looks foreign and ridiculous to her. What she knows is she has a need, and it should be tended to—by someone other than herself.

I see this energy pattern as having been more prevalent in the generations of women who preceded me than in the generation of which

I am a part or the generations that have come after me. They are the women who are built like distress signals. The ones who send out an SOS with the slightest provocation. She is not imagining a world that would ask her to show up large or independent. She is another easy target for feminism. She is the quintessential damsel in distress. The one who needs rescuing. The one who does not know how to get out of the lion's den on her own. The one who has a starring role in so many epic tales that are more about the hero and the dragons he slays than they are about the girl in the high tower. Still, the girl in the high tower gets consideration from me. I am less interested in how it undermines feminist politics and critique and more interested in how she got in the tower to begin with. Why is the Beggar Woman positioned so helplessly? Why does she always need saving? Why is she always without? And certainly, why can't she rescue her*self*?

I have known various renditions of the Beggar Woman. She is infrequent in my life, but she has shown up more than once. She is like the Willing Woman in that she angers those who fight to rewrite the feminine template into something powerful and capable and independent. And this revision is not because she isn't already capable of that. The revision is necessary—feminism is necessary—because women are so often made to appear small. But the Beggar Woman, unlike the Willing Woman, is not operating from obedience. The Beggar Woman is operating from need. My truth is that she understands neither her world nor her own capacity to move in it. She is not providing for herself. She is waiting on provisions to be made for her. And she *is* evidence of patriarchy in that she is so pervasive in our literature, in our film, that she has been crafted into our collective consciousness. Hers is a necessary position in order for a dominating idea about what it means to be masculine to be carried out.

The Beggar Woman is dealing in the deficits. I have a friend whose wife cannot drive, is scared of public transportation, is frequently unaware of how to get where she needs to go (geographically speaking), does not work, does not know how to cook, is paralyzed around decision-making, and is sexually stunted because she does not know what her own body likes nor does she know how to navigate determining what someone else likes. She is the one who screams and calls frantically for help when there's a fly in the room. Every time I am in her presence, she is asking for help with something—anything. She asks for help with little things that, from my perspective, can be easily managed without any outside assistance or guidance. She is so out of tune with herself and her environment that they have become foreign places to her. Things she feels she is at the whim and mercy of. And my friend is always there to rescue her. He is an enabler for sure and needs to feel needed, but her perpetual state of helplessness frustrates even him from time to time. She is not one to stand up confidently on her own.

For clarity, this is not a person who has anything pinning her to the ground like that. She is college educated and from a big family—a family in which she is the only girl. Her parents had seven children: six boys and one girl. The mother passed away when the girl was not yet three years old. She grew up under the direct care and influence of seven men, including her father. From what I am told, her only formal responsibility in that house was to learn how to comb her own hair. Everything else was done for her or on her behalf—everything. Meals were prepared. Laundry done. House cleaned. Errands run. Groceries bought and put away. She was taken everywhere she needed to go. She was handed money when she needed it. No one insisted she get an after-school job or learn to balance a checkbook. When she talked about employment, her father and brothers asked her how much money she needed and gave it. When she asked her father about learning how to drive, he filled her ear with statistics about how many car crashes there are in the United States every year and suggested that it would be safer for him to just drive her wherever she needed to go. There was a chore list that went up on the refrigerator every week. Her brothers all had tasks assigned to them. She did not. When she had trouble with schoolwork and needed help, one of her older brothers usually ended up doing the work *for* her rather than showing her how. She was *the princess,* and in this family, that designation came with the kind of privilege that is crippling. By the time she was in college, her sense of entitlement was the very thing that became a mushroom cloud of practiced (and encouraged) helplessness.

My friend met her just after her father died. She was flailing about dismally at the close of her senior year, and he saved her. He talks about how unaware and fledgling she was. He recognized it from across the room in the dining hall, and he was drawn to it because his own need to be the provider, the savior, the proverbial knight, made her an attractive choice. They've been married a long time. Her neediness floors me, as does his inclination to accommodate it.

The Beggar Woman is, in and of herself, needy, but the wider conversation is that her presentation is addressing a need—one that feeds into a certain kind of egoistic interpretation of what men are supposed to do. Here is where patriarchy and discussions about the masculine principle come into full view. Because the Beggar Woman's vulnerability seeks a hero. And in order for one to take on a heroic position, there is a necessary counterposition of vulnerability, helplessness, defenselessness, or shiftlessness to enact it. A hero needs to scale a wall. He needs to pull a maiden from a burning building. He needs to save her from the dragon. He needs an endangered species. But where the dynamic becomes problematic is in the exigency of codependence and prostration in the Beggar Woman. How broken down she has to be in order for rescue to be decreed. The hero needs the disabled, the forlorn, the inexpert, and the infirm in order to make true what he needs to believe about himself. If she is intact and capable, or, perhaps more to the point, aware of and responding to her capacity, then the hero has no one to save.

The Beggar Woman has bought into the idea that she cannot pull herself up on her own. She may even believe that it is not her work to do. She may believe that job belongs to someone else. I don't know the evolution of this pattern of behavior. In the case of my friend's wife, I connect it to her upbringing. How enlisted and prescribed her motionlessness seems to be. But I am sure it can emerge from other examples and experiences. It certainly is an old model. I am sure it can come from having tried to venture out in the interest of independence only to discover that you are untried and ill equipped for the experience. I suppose it can train self-reliance out of a person if the experience was particularly traumatic or perpetual. I am sure a person can start to adopt the idea that they need rescuing, even putting themselves in situations unconsciously or otherwise that make that philosophy feel true.

Every horror film, however contemporary or classic, seems to have a woman squealing and falling helplessly down when something scary or unusual shows up. She is standing when she should be running. She has the car keys in her hand, drops them, and then suddenly can't seem to figure out which key is the right key. She is watching the monster lumber toward her, and instead of opening the door and getting out of the way of danger, she is calling for help. Over and over again calling for help without recognizing that she has a way to rescue herself if she would but *move*. It is one of the most annoying cinematic ploys for me personally, and it is in almost every horror film, every action film, every dramatic film. There is always a Beggar Woman, caterwauling and begging for help instead of using her own resources.

I said at the beginning that this is not a holding pattern I see very much in real time in my own generation. And that is true. I do not have an abundance of experience with her, and I will admit to being glad about that. I suppose my own political leanings do not celebrate the woman who is ineffectual and incompetent. I do not believe the Beggar Woman is without resources or ability, and maybe that's why she is so difficult to empathize with. She is a woman who is deliberate about being stuck in order to affirm the need for chivalry. She is the woman who will stand in front of a puddle and feel stymied by it. As opposed to jumping over it, walking through it, or going around it, she will stand there, waiting for someone to come and throw their raincoat on top of it so she can move. It is an incapacitated position. And it does not have to be—at least, not from my perspective. I have known women who have encountered circumstances that reduced them to rubble. And in the hard moments they *were* temporarily debilitated—temporarily. I have known those moments myself. But the paralysis is finite. It certainly is not a place to hang your hat—not when there is so much life waiting for you, just as soon as you move.

One opposite consideration of the Beggar Woman that I want to offer though is around the idea of being able to ask for help. It seems to me that this woman has real proficiency here. I myself do not, and it has resulted in chaos and undue stress on so many occasions. The Beggar Woman is asking for help. She knows how to do it and do it again. I would posit that where she is out of balance is in asking too often. There is an unapplied effort attached to her supplications. I would further posit that she is asking for the wrong kind of help. She is looking for someone to pull her up and keep her up. The real work is in being able to ask for the kind of assistance that pulls you into your own resources, the kind that allows you to see the right answer as opposed to *giving* you the right answer. I do find value in the Beggar Woman's ability to ask for things. I need to practice that skill more—a lot more. And it is a skill. But so is resilience. So are self-awareness and self-reliance. In this regard, the Beggar Woman would do well to lean toward these things. If she does, she will not need rescuing. She will feel her own abundance, and she will know how to use it.

If you are creating from this energy pattern, what is at the front end of it could be feelings of incapability. Something in you is struggling to believe in your own capacity. In that regard, creativity probably stumbles forward in difficult fashion. You may feel clumsy in it. You probably are constantly crumbling up the pages you just wrote or sketched on, convinced they are not good enough. You may be a person who, in order to generate something, needs a lot of hand-holding in order to get it into the world. Needs someone who is telling you it's wonderful and to keep going. That someone is probably the person to come behind you and pluck what you discarded out of the trash can, smooth it out with their fingers and put it back in front you. Someone who is trying to save you from your own internal critic. Someone who, when you throw up your hands and declare that you can't do it, steadies your feet and insists that you can. You may find that without these people, you struggle to get anything out at all.

Attributes

- Helplessness
- Fear
- Codependence
- Doubt
- Or self-awareness

Exercise for the Beggar Woman

Write a story about a girl who needs saving. You determine what she needs to be sheltered or protected or rescued from. Let it be something you feel personally connected to. Something that lives in your body. Something you fret about or feel ill equipped to handle. Describe her predicament in as much detail as will give the widest sense of her torment.

Once you have that, write her a hero. Describe the hero. Take your time in doing so. Flesh this character all the way out. What do they look like? Give them a name. How do they speak? Describe the horse they rode in on, if that's your thing. Talk about how they save the girl. What form does their heroism take? What kind of hero does the girl need in order to be safe and standing entirely upright?

Once you are done with your story, and you have taken the time to flesh out what the hero is composed of, go back and erase the hero's name and write in your own. Read it aloud. Hear yourself being described so powerfully, so masterfully. Take note of how you imagine them and then imagine yourself that way. Recognize your own ability to step into the very things you wrote for someone else. You can practice being your own savior. You can. You can don their costume. You can use their language, their wisdom, their bravery, their moxie. It all came from you, after all. You can write yourself out of the tower and onto dry land. You can write yourself as a woman who will try everything before deciding she needs help. Practice it. After a while, you will start to like how it feels.

If you identify as the version of the Beggar Woman who finds it difficult to ask for help, try this: Write down the things/circumstances/individuals that are in the way of your ability to name what you need or to seek help. Once you have generated your list, speak directly to those things, telling them to move off the path. For example, "To my own stubborn heart, my sometimes obstinate brain, to the stories I have made up about how strong I have to be; listen. Move away from here. I have a right to name what I need, quietly, and aloud." And then name it! Name what you need. Practice the saying of it. Practice honoring yourself for being a woman who knows how to honor her most fragile parts.

Examples of This Archetype

Even a casual perusal of literature and film will give you a cornucopia of examples. The Beggar Woman is Rapunzel and Snow White and Cinderella. She is Lois Lane and Olive Oyl and Mary Jane Watson in *Spider-Man.* She is every girl who acted in King Kong films, remakes included. She is usually smart and yet somehow in trouble over and over again.

I have noticed a trend, though, whereby the woman who is perpetually vulnerable and needy, by the end of some films, has discovered some spunk and is suddenly picking up weapons or turning and confronting her fear as opposed to screaming for help. That evolution, however gimmicky, always makes me smile. The Beggar Woman has her hand out, but it is clear that if she elects to, she can ball it into a fist. She can dig inside her own pockets. She can surprise herself by discovering how deep they actually are.

fifteen

The Bone Woman

Why you always lookin' back, woman? Leave the dead alone.

Bone Woman

Because you are the bone woman
A blood-borne basket of wind
And thirst . . .

Because you are looking for your missing
Limbs in an ocean
That will not acknowledge your name
It does not know your name . . .

The shriek in your belly
Is an ancestral rumble
A deep and wanting thing
A lost love whose hands
Are always at your throat . . .

You do not mind the tugging

Because you were born
Knowing your mouth
Would be a landing place—
A whistle stop
For songs you've can't get back . . .

Because you are the bone woman,

You are inclined to haunt
Your own body.

Because you are the bone woman
You do not bury

Your dead.

The Bone Woman is a swiveled neck. Her eyes are keen on what is behind her. She will not leave it behind her. She pulls it up from where it is and sets it down on her lap. She does this upon waking. She is the keeper. The one holding on. The one who can't let go. The one whose memories have been fashioned into nooses. The one who cannot hold today in her hands, because they are spilling over with yesterday. The one whose commitment to the past is explicit. The one who keeps herself like a mausoleum. The one who drags the bones around. The one who lets every skeleton have a dance. She does not ask them to live in the closet. They are permitted to clutter up the living room, to keep her up at night.

The Bone Woman is doubled over in the past. It is so present with her, it is the *only* present *for* her. Something in her needs to hold on. She is a collector. She holds onto yesterday because it gives her an identity. She has come to believe it serves her in some way. There's an ironic continuum in that she keeps hold of everything, even the hurt—especially the hurt—because she has come to believe that it arms her to keep it nearby. She has catalogued every moment, every wrong turn, every missed opportunity, every miscalculation and misstep. She fixates on them. She has a misapplied relationship with the past. She has no relationship at all with letting go.

The Bone Woman will not bury the dead. She is a veritable graveyard of memory. She holds the bones of former lovers. The bones of her children when they were small. The bones of her childhood and her parents and what they said and how they went. She holds the bones of old disagreements. The bones of degrees not earned. Things she sacrificed and compromised. She holds the bones like they are the most expensive part of her. They are crackling with age, insistent on decomposition, yet she dusts them off daily, spreads them out around the room, lets each one be a part of the now. The effort is rigorous and exhausting. But she does it. She does it religiously.

I would posit that the Bone Woman keeps time with the past because she can control its application. The present is not a thing she feels ready to manage, but the past is now a rock in her pocket. She could take it out and throw it, but she elects instead to keep it, to hold it in her hand, to let it weigh her down. She regards the rock as an anchor, a way to keep both feet firmly on the ground. She does not realize she has the right to be boundless and that the ways in which she holds onto the past limit her ability to move purposefully into the future or to be fully present in the now.

She makes up stories about what yesterday looked like. I do not intend for that to sound synonymous with lying. That's not the business end of it. No, I think the Bone Woman is subject to hyperbolic versions of an old story. The breakup with someone is held in her memory as an epic romance with a tragic end, a Romeo and Juliet revisioning for an ordinary encounter that ended. The days when she was young and more able to frolic are repackaged in her brain as much more magical and awe-inspiring than they were in real time.

The Bone Woman is scared letting go will feel like losing. She hasn't yet reckoned with the notion that there is victory in saying good-bye. It is not the equivalent of forgetfulness. It is not synonymous with denial or repressed feelings. It is always important to gather up what you hold in your body, unpack it, feel it all the way through, process why you carry it the way you do, make determinations about what serves you and what does not. And it is important to be able and *willing* to let go of that which does not serve you, that which keeps you smothered under the weight of all those yesterday stories. The ability to say a proper good-bye leaves you with enough space in your ribcage to receive whatever is awaiting you. If you are wallowing at the gravesides of the not yet buried, you cannot even recognize what the *living* are doing.

The Bone Woman, in some respects feels like an old familiar character to me. I have a cultural reference for her as well. If she is operating with diligence, she looks like so many elders I know who are peripatetic in keeping the dead around. They are elegies and altars and old photos. They have deep investments in the ancestral realm. They do not let those who *were* exist only in *was,* if that makes sense. They call out to their ancestors. They speak their names. They tell their stories. They speak them into existence as a deliberate daily practice. The distinction for me between that and what the Bone Woman reflects when she is out of balance is in remembering the past as opposed to hoarding it. Remembrance is powerful, necessary. It is grounding and instructive. It offers a wealth of clarity about the now. Hoarding is something else entirely. Hoarding the past is reflective of a wound.

The Bone Woman, as I have seen her most pervasively, is carrying an emptiness. She is trying to fill it with yesterdays that do not help her flourish in today. In my mind, so much of what drives her behavior is rooted in projection. She has opted (probably unconsciously) to idealize or demonize images and individuals from her past. She is allowing them to have so much weight and precedence in her life. If she is idealizing the past and thusly keeping it around, she has made a commitment to believing things were so much better way back when. The present holds no music for her. She can't hear it at all. So she beckons yesterday to be available. She ties a bow around it, decorates it in her mind, and convinces herself that every day before today looked like Christmas. That is projection, not reality. If she is demonizing images and individuals from her past, she is electing to use it all as a landing place for blame and hurt as opposed to acknowledging any deficiency in herself. Whatever happened in the past is the culprit keeping her from having a full and complete life. This is the story she has made up.

To add such hyperbole to the past, whether glorious or pejorative, is an effort to have control. She needs her judgments about what happened. She needs her revisions. Without them she would have to stand inside of right now and see what she has made of herself. And there is likely to be a lot of fear and hurt, shame, and blame staring back at her.

My grandmother occupied this space a good deal of her life. At least, in my experience of her, this seems to be a true statement. She held onto everything—every single thing. She and my grandfather could have a disagreement, and before the thesis statement about what generated it could emerge, my grandmother would start talking about something that happened in the 1930s. They had been married for sixty years, had two children, buried one, educated countless, and yet when my grandmother was upset, she always worked her way back to events that happened before any of us were in the world—before they were even married. She held so much resentment around things in the past that she would not let them leave. She kept them nearby, like a switchblade in her pocketbook. Soon as she felt confronted, disappointed, or hurt, out came an old wound, one she polished and repolished before brandishing it like a weapon. And as much as it annoyed or disrupted my grandfather, it was clear that the one who was bleeding out was my grandmother. Clear to everyone but her.

For the Bone Woman, keeping the past around is not a mindful practice, as it is for the Third Eye Woman, though she does it intentionally. The Bone Woman believes it gives her a sense of her reality, but for me, what sounds truer is that she is conceiving of her reality through a lens muddied with too many old stories. It's all black-and-white photos and unreliable memory that she has constructed into a mission statement about holding on. I say unreliable memory because when you carry long-ago wounding around with you that way, you've limited your ability to see it for what it is and what it is not. It starts to become the stuff of imagination and, yes, projection.

My grandmother did not want to let go of old hurt. I don't think she felt she got her just reward around it or that the people who caused the hurt were appropriately "punished," so she kept it around because it lived in her body as an unfinished thing. What the Bone Woman struggles to see is that *she* is the finisher. She is the one who is positioned to punctuate those sentences. She is the one who must insist on a proper burial, and that burial can't be tied to anyone outside of herself. No strategy is successful if, in order for you to be okay, you require other people to change. There's no guarantee that they will, and in the case of the Bone Woman, these people or circumstances may be long gone or have no memory of the thing she is clutching with both hands. More than once I saw my grandfather look genuinely baffled at a reference my grandmother made to something that he had long ago forgotten. It did not occupy any space in his consciousness, which only served to anger my grandmother more because her relationship to it was vast.

I liken the Bone Woman, in some ways, to a bag lady. She is lugging around suitcases filled with clothes that do not fit her anymore. She takes them everywhere she goes. She complains from back pain; that pain comes from carrying the baggage, but she makes no correlation between the two. She is exhausted from carrying it all, but she will not put down her bags. She does not even bother to sort through what she has packed inside. But she believes she needs them. She has been caught without something to wear before, and she will not let that happen again. She is resentful of the people around her who seem so much lighter, the ones who do not seem to carry around as much. When they tell her she should get rid of her baggage, she believes they are trying to take something from her. And though so much of what she's packed is out of season, too big, or too small, she wants them to believe that the stuff inside *matters.* She has let it come to mean so much to her. She is angered when they cannot connect to it. She is sad that they cannot connect to it.

That is analogous to hoarding. The ritual is the backbreaking kind. I think a lot about the business of not letting go of the past. How taxing it is for some. How much it pulls you out of your body. How much it corrupts the present. How tainted the lens can become. There are things I continue to carry, long-ago yesterday things. There are things I carry that are not even mine—stories I heard that changed the topography of my spirit. So much of that lives in my writing now, though. Stories about my family's history, its migration from the South, what my grandfather sacrificed, what my grandmother gave, how my mother grew up, how her brother died, even historical reference points like what happened to Emmett Till and Medgar Evers, and the four little girls who died in the bombing of the Sixteenth Street Baptist Church—all yesterday stories I held in my body and never let go of.

But there were other things too: Things that didn't let any daylight in. Autobiographical things. Personal things. Things I witnessed as a child. Friends I lost to gun violence and incarceration. My stepfather. My stepfather. My stepfather—he was a dragon difficult to slay. I had to knuckle in around it. I carried memories of him and that house for a long time. And I carried them like a bit in my mouth, like a noose, like a cross. I carried them badly. I carried them often. I think I did that because they allowed me to stay broken, and something in me believed I was supposed to be broken. They enabled me to be tragic, and for a while I was sure that's who I was. So I clung to them.

But my God, it was a dysfunctional relationship with the past. I was pulling up the bones of a man who had been dead for decades just to let him (his memory) pulp me one more time. I kept pulling up his bones, lacerating myself on them. Everywhere I went I was bleeding. And I was doing it to myself.

Listen, did my stepfather impact my growth and development? Absolutely. Did I deserve to remember what it was like to be in his house? Yes. Was it necessary for me to give him a starring role in my adulthood? To inform the ideas I had about myself? Hell, no. Not at all.

I had to practice letting go. It took some time. I don't have grave-digger advice on this one; you know, just put him back in the ground, cover him up, and walk away. No, it wasn't as straight a line as that. I had to first put my hands into the muck and muddle of *why* I kept digging him up. Why I was so committed to brokenness. How I came to believe such ridiculous lies about myself. When I was on the other side of that soul work, burying that man was easy.

I don't think about him much anymore. And when I do, anger is not what comes up. It's mostly sadness—*for him* and certainly for the little girl I was. But I have gone back and fetched her. She is all right now. Her magic and resilience serve me well in the now. And I am in the *now*—the *right* now and in this very moment now. Yes, memory can be slick. It can slip into the room, a midnight ghost that catches you unaware. But I am better about putting things where they belong. I know how to bury the dead.

If you are the Bone Woman, you are deeply involved with yesterday, what it held, who it held. But the notion that you can control it by keeping it around is a false notion. Letting it take up more space in your house than the present does not serve you, not ultimately. The stories you've made up about its necessity are just that: stories you've made up. You are not as true as you can be if you choose to let some of it go.

I'm not positing all of it should leave. Some of it may, in fact, be useful to you. Some of it may be remarkable in keeping you familiar with what you've come through, the roads you've traveled, all of the ways you have loved and lost. But you cannot direct bones to do anything other than clutter up and clang along your right-now, could-be life. Bones are evidence that something has *departed.* There was an exit. Let it be an exit. Let the bones be the bones. Do not try to reanimate them. Do not decorate your home with them. Do not let them become a gated community that keeps you from yourself. Instead, seek an authentic life. A living life. A living life.

If you are trying to create from this energy pattern, what is at the front end of it is probably longing. And maybe regret. Something about you wants a do-over. Something about the past cajoles you, even if it is something negative (as in the case of my stepfather). There is a perceived reward for you in lugging those bodies around. You've been doing it so long you no longer notice the stench of decomposition. But you can deal rightly with your impressions. You can create in a way that lifts the fog. You can leave the past on the canvas. Let it moan and bleat there. Let it leap and dance there. You can unpack the baggage and sift through it in the writing, in the painting, in the drawing and sketching, in the sculpting. You can let your art serve as a final resting place for the bones. You can let your art be the door closing. Let it be the final farewell.

Attributes

- Controlling
- Regretful
- Elegiac
- Wistful

Exercise for the Bone Woman

First I offer a story I heard years ago: the story of two monks. These monks were on a pilgrimage of sorts to find and then honor a relic of a saint. During the course of their travel, they happened upon a river where they saw a young woman sitting before it, weeping. She was afraid to cross the river on her own. She asked the monks if they would carry her across. The younger one refused and turned away from her; because of their discipline, they were not permitted to touch women. The older one, however, picked the woman up without hesitation or conversation, carried her across the river, and set her down on the other side.

As the monks kept walking, the older one walked steadily, taking in his surroundings and the experience with real joy. He was entirely present. The younger was sullen, moody, and distracted. When he could not hold it any longer, he erupted. He admonished the older monk and reminded him of the rule that pertained to not touching women. The younger one went on and on about the other carrying the woman, and the older one listened quietly. When the younger monk was finished, the older monk told him, "All I did was carry her across the river. You have been carrying her all day."

Write the eulogy for the Bone Woman. Write the eulogy for the things you have been carrying around, the things you have not let go of, the bones you have not buried. Write the eulogy for what should be allowed to depart.

Take inventory of what those things are. Identify that which should be permitted to leave. Let it be praise-heavy if that is how you carry it. Let it be a truthful depiction of what that thing or person meant to you. If it was not positive, let the praise exist in the fact that they are finally going underground. Let the praise exist in the notion that their bones will not clutter up your hallway anymore. You will have room to hang new pictures, to sweep out the dust that yesterday brought. Praise the saying of good-bye. Remember that good-bye has its place. Assemble the bones that do not belong in your living life and write them into ashes.

Now, for the things that you wish to keep, the things that do not deter you from the present, build an altar space. In the writing, build a sacred place where all of these memories can be kept. Write them into pretty glass jars. Write them into ornate curio cabinets. Write them onto tall, tall shelves that you will dust off once a month. You can keep them nearby, but they do not need to occupy your body. No, your body belongs to today.

Examples of This Archetype

In Amy Tan's novel *The Joy Luck Club,* the character Auntie Ying-ying is presented as a tragic figure who lived most of her life with deep regret and sadness about the past. An abused woman who killed her infant son in China when she was out of her mind with grief over how her husband was treating her, she never left the scene of the crime. She left her husband. She left China. But she could not fully depart from what happened to her and what she had done in her past. As a result, she was scarcely mentally or emotionally present or available to her daughter. She remained woefully in memory, and it had very real grip on her. It restricted her capacity to move forward. It did not leave her with enough stuff left in her gut to offer anything substantive to her child or her new husband. When she finally comes into this clarity, she is galvanized by a need to offer her daughter something made of more backbone. She sees how her entanglement with the past is setting her daughter up to be equally tragic and stuck. For me, Ying-ying's awakening is tectonic. How she begins taking ownership of her story. How she begins to finally and bravely bury her dead.

Another literary character who juts out for me in this regard is Sethe in the Toni Morrison novel *Beloved*. She is entirely haunted by her past. Born a slave on a Kentucky plantation, she knew the horrors of violation and abuse before running away to Ohio, along with her children. Sethe could not shake the memories of the things that happened to her. The lynching of her mother. The boys who held her down in the barn and robbed her of her breast milk. The subsequent lashes she took when she told on them. The day "School Teacher," the man whose cruelty she ran from back in Kentucky, found her in Ohio. How she took her children into the woodshed and tried to kill all four (succeeding in killing one) to keep them from being taken back to that plantation. She keeps all of those parts of the past close to her. Jugular close. She is a woman who is enslaved by the past, by the skeletal fragments of all that happened to her, and what she did, and what it left her with.

Morrison describes Sethe as a person who could not get the past to leave her be. It crowded in on her. It forced its way into everything. It did not permit her passage. At the end of the novel, when Sethe is finally and authentically mourning the loss of the daughter she killed, her lamentation is "She [the daughter] is my best thing." Paul D, a man who came off of the same plantation and finds her in Ohio more than a decade after she has run off and subsequently murdered her child, corrects Sethe and gives her the best bit of clarity I know. He tells her, "You your best thing, Sethe. You are."

Bone Woman, Paul D is right. The past is not your best thing. It is not your only thing. Fundamentally, *you* are what you need to hold onto—you.

sixteen

The **Liberator** Woman

She the Underground Railroad. She the freedom train.

Some mornings shudder into me
Slick as butter
And sweet.
And I feel all of me . . .

My flat feet
The ocean water in my belly
Swallowin' everything I can't eat.

I feel my neck poked up
Like early spring buds

My hips be wind chimes
My back the widest road.

I could stay in the fullness of me
All day just let the sun lap
Up my bones

But I can't find no music
By myself for myself.

I need to bring folks
With me into dawn plucked
Symphonies like Sunday morning

Choir ladies findin' God
In the hymnal

I go lookin' for the lost ones

The stolen ones

The captured ones

I go lookin' for 'em
Til they know they free.

I just be lookin' for 'em
Til they know
They free . . .

The Liberator Woman is activated. She is a sledgehammer slicing off the shackle. A bandit queen seizing liberty in both hands. The moonlight requisitioner. The one who exonerates and unrestrains. She is not a philanthropist. She is not being charitable. Her hands are in it. Her head is in it. Her heart is in it. She cannot move in the world the way she needs to if she perceives of injustice. Injustices do not allow for a limitless existence for others—most especially for people she feels a kinship with, people she loves.

The Liberator Woman is willing to forego any advantage she may have to pull others out of a disadvantaged space. She is hypersensitive to the suffering of others, whether they are consciously aware of that suffering or not. In my experience, her concern about the liberation of others is rooted in her own experience with constricting circumstances. She knows how metal bites into flesh. She knows what a trench feels like. She is familiar with solitary confinement. She has known the stink of deprivation. How it clings to the skin. How it collides with reason. How it wants to turn the bones to soup.

All of my personal experience with her bears this out. She loathes the oppressive politic that seeks to silence expression and rob individuals of what sovereignty they should have over themselves. She fixates on the problems inherent in hierarchical power structures. She is certain that each should receive a proper share. Her blood moves with the idea that freedom is *not* metaphorical, not a privilege offered to the few. In fact, she is certain that freedom cannot be offered at all. We come into the world with it. It's a birth right. A human right. A divine right. And while she cannot author it for anyone, she is committed to guiding people toward a more liberated existence.

Now, because language is sometimes a conflict of opposites, it's important to distinguish between freedom and liberty to ripen awareness about what catalyzes the Liberator Woman to show up the way she does.

Conversations about freedom and liberty are thematic for Americans. We grow up singing anthems about freedom and liberty. We memorize facts about the Statue of Liberty and what a beacon she is of "Bring me your tired, your poor . . ." We learn about Patrick Henry and the famous speech he made to the Virginia Convention wherein he decries apathy and proclaims, "Give me liberty or give me death!" Our founding documents extol the rights of man and the virtues of independence. And being a colored girl in this country, I have certainly grappled with the pervasive languaging and mislanguaging of what it means to be free and what it means to be liberated. As much as the African American community (as I have lived and experienced it) invokes words like *freedom,* it is an elusive idea for so many of us. Elusive because we talk about it as though it is a mythical creature that lives in the abstract. Lives in the hypothetical. Lives only to avail itself to the privileged sect.

Because in this country, the legacy of chattel slavery has so informed my ideas about race and isms, and because the representation of enslaved folk always had them hoping and praying that one day *Massa* might *give* them their freedom, and because I heard the words *freedom* and *liberty* used interchangeably, it was a long process for me to deconstruct the dialectic and emerge with my head above water. Simply put, freedom is inside, liberty is outside. Freedom is the stuff of your marrow. It is as attached to you as your DNA. Liberty pertains to a sensory-based reality, one that is reliant upon flesh and feeling. Liberty is about the absence of literal restraint—a roadblock, a jail cell, a prison yard, barbed wire fences, a locked door, shackles and chains and handcuffs, a muzzle, an armed guard, a solitary-confinement unit.

The Liberator Woman is concerned with freedom, but she is organized around liberty. The distinction between the two is critical to understanding her. The Liberator Woman is not trying to lead anybody to freedom. She knows she can't. Her work lies in liberation. The Liberator Woman is the one who stretches her limbs around social justice activism. She is not a liberal in this regard; she is a radical. She does not wish to engage in some long-winded treatise about ideologies and philosophies and not move. She does not wish to postulate or theorize unless there is action at the end. She sees an unjust system, and she wants to snatch it down brick by brick. She recognizes a trend in legislation that encourages mass incarceration for black and brown boys at numbers disproportionate to the population, and she is scheming. She wants to see the thing topple. She is the woman who will smuggle the prisoners out. The one who will loosen the cuffs. The one who cuts the barbed wire. The one who unlocks the deadbolt.

She is so boundless she wants others to feel it too. She is frustrated by how difficult it is to convince people of their own right to it. She studies the psychology of the oppressed. She knows what it is like to believe you were born with your back bent in servitude. She knows the fiction it generates in the brain. She has a mission statement written in the blood of West Africans whose bones litter the bottom of the Atlantic. She has a mission statement written in the foot stomp and fight of the Zapatista movement by the women in Chiapas. Her liberation marches on in the context of the wider community: the women who scratched and clawed in this country to change legislation that restricted their movements. The Liberator Woman is likely a feminist. A womanist. An activist. She challenges the construct, and she does so knowing it is sometimes no different than dangling your flesh before wolves.

She challenges limiting circumstances as much as limiting beliefs. She is the woman who grabs you by the arm and asks you what the hell you're thinking. She shows you an escape route. She insists on you taking it. The Liberator Woman can be coarse. The business of extricating someone from behind enemy lines is not for the faint of heart. She borrows from the example of Moses. She is willing to stand before the sea with her arms open, her people behind her. She is willing to walk by faith and work. She knows what it is to have to tug and scrap to convince people of their right to an unrestricted life. She has seen too often, has felt it herself, how confinement can start to feel like home. Like a thing you deserve. Like a legacy. Like the only thing you know.

It's tricky. The Liberator Woman is clear that confining circumstances are easier to manage when they are external than when they are internal. Prisons exist not because of the metal and steel holding bodies behind them. It's not the guards or the guns. The Liberator Woman understands that prisons require agreement. Each body confined to a cage is a person who has been positioned to concede or agree to their confinement. That is not an agreement of the flesh; it is an agreement in the mind. The same mechanism is at work in confining circumstances that may not be mapped out in cell bars and barbed wire. They are mapped out in poverty and mediocre schools. They are mapped out in the limiting beliefs that become so endemic in the oppressed, in what they come to think about themselves and their opportunities.

I knew young black boys in 1993, during what came to be called the Summer of Violence in northeast Denver, whose belief that their survival was improbable was so acute that they walked into Pipkin Mortuary, a then-struggling business, and paid for their funerals in advance. They felt pinned in and frustrated by what their realities held for them. They responded to their experience by fully integrating the idea that they were not supposed to have agency, not supposed to be liberated and unconfined. That belief makes a prisoner faster than shackles ever have. The Liberator Woman understands that. She is galvanized by the potential for emancipation. She is willing to spill her own flesh to make it real for as many people as she can. She believes she owes it. She believes she is inconvenienced by that kind of suffering in others. She is not a Samaritan so much as she is a firewalker. And in that she is committed.

There was a woman in my community who walked this way. She had been born into formidable circumstances. Abandoned by her mother, her father never involved, she was shuffled from group home to foster care to group home. She had not been shown kindness in those places. She was often hungry and terrified and alone. Her childhood felt like a prison sentence for her. And she believed in her circumstances. She believed it was all that should be offered to a black girl whose own parents did not care enough to stick around. But she graduated from high school and was afforded the opportunity to go to school in Nairobi.

While she was there, she learned about Frantz Fanon and writings that described the arduous process of emancipating the mind. She felt herself moving in concert with this new awareness. She was becoming something larger, clearer. She thought about how the context she was born into combined with the language that was used conveyed a message to her that she was inferior, that she was not supposed to know a liberated life. In recognizing the mythology in it all, she stepped into herself with a new kind of clarity—the kind that showed her how much of the lie she had ingested. How she had come dangerously close to setting up her life as one of the captured ones. She was grateful to know the fire in her belly. She made it her mission to ignite that fire in others who were still wallowing in misery. She threw her knuckles into that work and lifted so many people out of the quicksand. The business of liberation was her identity. She went into war zones and gang-infested communities. She went into crack houses and tenements. She was the Liberator Woman. I never saw her be anything but that.

When the Liberator Woman is out of balance, she is probably at risk for stretching herself out so far for others that she neglects her own life.

She is always going back into the trenches to lift out another body. She can forget the fact that she herself belongs in the sun, that the daylight she is trying so valiantly to make available to others should be permitted to touch her too. She can lose sight of her own right to abundance. She can forget to remember her own bright kingdom, to keep her own mouth wet with smiling. People who devote themselves to serving the needs of others are always at risk of neglecting themselves. It seems to be an occupational hazard. In her push to offer goodness to everyone else, she should remember to leave something left for herself.

If you are creating from this energy pattern, what is at the front end of it is an acute sense of justice. You are using your art to generate a grand becoming for others. You are trying to get folks off the plantation with your art. You are creating to lift the veil, to open eyes, to bring people into awareness of what shackles may bind them, and to get them to shake it off. You create to show folks what freedom looks like, how much daylight we have in our possibilities. You are saying, "Come on, children. Let's go. The North Star is this way. I can show you where your magic is. I can show you how good it feels to let go your limbs toward dancing. It's this way. It's over here. Let's go!"

Attributes

- Activist
- Socially responsible
- Devoted
- Progressive

Exercise for the Liberated Woman

Write a story or a poem in which you find a letter that begins with the line: "This is the way to freedom." What does the letter say? Who is it addressed to? What *are* the directions to freedom? What does it feel like to find it? To know right where it is? To know it belongs to you?

Write it using a word pool. I offer these ten words as a way in: *continents, swoop, music box, swoon, zeal, honeyed, palpitate, metronome, foolproof, parable.*

If none of the words resonate, pick ten of your own from a dictionary. Be random about it. Flip through the pages and wherever your eyes fall first, write that word down. Your consciousness will tell you how to use them.

Describe the road to *freedom.* Freedom is your birthright. Liberty is largely about circumstance. In my experience, the Liberator Woman would benefit from being deliberate about regarding her freedom and what it consists of constantly. It can serve as a powerful reminder that while on the quest to liberate others, the ultimate expression of love and service is to be deeply involved in one's own freedom and to never lose sight of it, or one's own rightful place in the sun. Remember, freedom happens from the inside. Almost everything does.

Examples of This Archetype

Harriet Tubman is an obvious example of the Liberator Woman. She escaped from slavery and felt compelled to sneak back onto plantations to liberate countless others from slavery. She could have chosen to rest comfortably in her own liberation, but for her, the fullness of that experience could only be reached if she helped others know it for themselves.

I think Susan B. Anthony is another good example. She grew up in a Quaker family that had long traditions in activism. She felt that zeal for justice, and it catalyzed her to join the women's rights movement and finally the suffrage movement. But she was also interested in and fought for the abolition of slavery, as well as a woman's rights to vote, hold property, and keep her earnings. Her identity, like Harriet Tubman's, was about liberating others—most often at great risk to herself.

seventeen

The Woman of **Words**

She got somethin' to say. And she gon say it.

Some women know what words are for . . .
They slide them around their teeth
Chew through the words
Til the words believe them
Lift their tongues from a watery grave
Put flesh back in the bones . . .

What would we be without the stories?
The pulled up parts of who we were
Stretched out in hallelujahs
And lord-have-mercy . . .

There are women who know how to stitch
Us back together
How to tell us what happened and
Who did it . . .
How to steal rivers and
Starve silence.

There are women who remember the world
When it was new and slick and
Bubbling over in delicious.
They tell us how we died
They tell us we never die

There are villages at the bottom of their soup pots
They are witch-medicine wonderful . . .

An untied bundle of mountain and stone.

Bring us the stories, woman.
Let us hold them in our hands.
Let us keep them under our tongue.
Let us suck out the venom of an undeclared life . . .

Bring us the stories, woman.
Until we know them for ourselves.

The Woman of Words is fat with narrative and lexicon. She is thick with remembered accounts. She is bubbling over in the telling and retelling of things and people and places and the long-ago stories of us. And the right-now stories of us. She is a listening potion. She is a rocking chair on a front porch, shelling peas and bringing the fruit of an old, old tale. She is dependent on getting all that memory to fit in her mouth. She is dependent on an audience. She is a voice that is steeped in superconsciousness. Her discourse is the song at the end of the world. Her discourse is the song that saves the world. It is the first and last big gift.

I've referenced the weight of an oral tradition several times over the course of writing this book, but here, in the Woman of Words, it gets to stretch out. Because storytelling is power. It is a way in to ourselves. A way to map out our experience. A way to find each other in the dark and to know all of our names. Storytelling gives us a way to remember what we did not know. And storytelling is medicine too.

My community lost a Woman of Words several years ago to cancer. The first time I met her, when she came to visit my school, I was ten years old. Opalanga Pugh was a woman built like a sycamore tree, over six feet tall, dark brown skin, garbled and weather whipped. She wore a turban and smiled through picket-fence teeth, a big gap between the front two. She was the first and only black woman I ever saw in my entire educative experience who was positioned as an authority. (The norm was nuns and priests.) She held the room in the web she spun. Story after story, some laced with song and chant. I was so transfixed by her I don't remember breathing. What I knew was that she was giving me—giving all of us—something important. Something we could *use*. Something that could make our bodies make sense. Something that made my grandparents more visible to me. Something that made my mama seem even more magic. Story after story. Creation stories. Human stories. Stories where animals got to be more cunning than man. Stories that explained ocean and rock. She lifted my spirit to exclamation. It was remarkable to watch her give the words their due—to show us, more than tell us. She surrounded us in stories that for me felt like lifelines.

When I became an adult, I had opportunity to know her and work with her. When I was working with students from Sub-Saharan Africa, she came and shared her stories with them. In the three weeks of countless workshops, immersions, school visits, and symposiums these students experienced, I never saw them as engaged or moved as when they were watching Opalanga spin stories into psalms, into history lessons, into legacy.

The Woman of Words knows that history and memory are reliant upon the stories that get passed. She submerges her bones in them. She engages them. She interacts with them. She knows that the more you listen to the stories, the more you pay attention to them, the more they start to stare back at you. Stories offer instruction, clarity, guidance. They serve as warnings, celebrations. The organizing principles of any society are in the stories its citizens use to tell themselves who they are. And in the stories they use to illustrate who the "other guy" is. And who the enemy is, and who God is, and who the gods and goddesses and sacred figures are, and what battles were lost but valiantly fought, and what wars were won, and who the heroes were.

The Woman of Words is transmuting history and heritage in the stories she tells. She is showing you what the land looked like before you
got here, how your grandfather got that hairline, how your grandmother
induced herself into labor by eating collard greens and watermelon,
how your family came to the city you were born in, how your sister
coveted you when you were an infant. Each strand is a road, and the
road is anthropomorphic, giving you whole volumes of yourself you
did not know were there.

My grandfather was my hero. Still is. Hearing stories about his upbringing gave me the widest sense of where I come from. How his mother hid
him under her wide skirts when the train she was on was robbed, how
he raised chickens in his yard and gave each one formal names, how he
played sandlot ball and helped his daddy paint houses, how his daddy
built the house he grew up in, how his sisters were all married and out of
the house before he was in the world, and how his five older brothers were
so epic and large, the way so many Southern men seemed to be. In all of
these stories I saw my own passage. I could track it, I could remember it,
I could share it with my own children. I could point to an image in an
old photo album and say, "Now this is your Uncle Mark. Mark Theodore
Roosevelt Johnson. I met him when I was a baby. . . ." It always seems that
the more I know of these stories, the more *me* I am. The more I understand about what that *me* is—what it consists of, how thick it is.

The Woman of Words keeps the language as a way to keep us whole,
as a way to hand us the music of our pulse and to remind us how old
that music is. The steady march of our lived experience can sometimes
train us in how to be unreal. We are so busy in our jobs and our parent-
ing and our responsibilities that we are at risk of being pulled out of
the wealth of who we are. We can feel besieged by it all. The Woman
of the Words wants you to sit on her porch, swing your feet out from
under you, and keep your ears open. She will tell you about the women
who looked something like you, who tied their babies on their backs
and worked the fields and factories—the ones who were wet nurses,
the ones who were wives and the ones who were not, the ones whose

resilience you inherited right along with the dimple in your left cheek. You can listen to the stories about who they were and how they moved, and let them straighten your spine. Let them illuminate for you, your own deep-river resources.

The Woman of Words loves a good story. If she is out of balance, this can make her quite the gossip. She can be fixed on the movements of others, real or perceived. She can be unconstrained in conversation and attach a narrative to an individual that is not possessing of accurate information. There is something seductive about gossip. It takes one piece of information and attaches it to the nearest thing your brain can find to concoct a story out of it. I would posit that not all gossip comes from a nefarious place. Some of it is unintentional misinformation. Some of it is more about assumption and projection than anything else.

I have experienced it in the context of performing. When you are on stage and you do something that moves someone else, often times they start projecting onto you. They see who they imagine you are based on what they heard you say. They believe they know something about your life and your politics. In some cases they have been forward enough to share those projections with me afterward, and I take the opportunity to correct them. In other cases, the stories that listeners make up catch up with me after they are already in the ethers. I know the mechanism well. It no longer surprises me, and more often than not it just sounds like the narrative they needed to believe. Gossip in its most noble form relies on projection. In its most insidious form, it is standardized in lies and half-truths.

Gossip is not concerned with the passing on of stories in the interest of legacy. It is interested in being provocative and keeping things in the wind. But gossip *is* a kind of storytelling, and I have had as much experience with the Woman of Words in balance as the storyteller as I have with her out of balance as the gossip. Both know the weight of words; the distinction lies, obviously, in intent.

Language is the carrier of culture. It is voluminous and ever changing. I think about the passing down of stories that stretch across so many continental shifts and cultural evolutions. I think about the bodies of Africans in the bellies of slave ships and how I have never heard the passing down of stories about the Middle Passage. How there are so many stories about plantation life and cotton fields and sugarcane and the way it bites into your palms. So many stories about the lash and the bullwhip, and families and land, and overseers, and the songs slaves sang and the meetings they held, and on and on, but nothing about the Middle Passage. There is a deliberate omission of those stories. And with so many other stories with so much blood on them, that omission tells me that the Middle Passage must have held unspeakable, nameless horror. For it to be so eradicated from the mouths of my ancestors, to be so buried and unoffered. What we know of it comes in the form of statistics and sterile information. But sometimes stories can emerge out of the ones that are so deliberately *untold*. There is that too.

The Woman of Words is a study in oral tradition. Whether the stories are her own or others, she speaks them into existence. She wants them to fit well in your ears. She wants you to keep them with you, to repeat them, to know they are large and important. She is the speaker, the teacher, the orator, the open mouth. She will tell you and tell you and tell you. She is wider than any textbook could be. She is the Woman of Words, and she is put here—put here to speak.

If you are creating from this energy pattern, then you are right where you need to be. Your art is a story quilt. You are weaving what stories you carry in the work you do. You are creating to tell these stories—your story. You know how important it is to speak and speak again. Your creative process is an extension of the stories and the inclination to share them. The storyteller's heart is an old, old tale. Let your art make us know it well.

Attributes

- Vivid
- Memory keeper

- Interested
- Curious

Exercise for the Woman of Words

Tell an untold story. Think about your family's history and what you know of it. Think of the details provided to you and by whom. What questions did their story leave you with? What sounded unsaid to you? Perhaps it's a detail you wanted to know that they didn't have. Tell *that* story. Tell the story you don't know.

Let your imagination gallop here. Use what you do know to write what you don't know. For example, I don't know a whole lot about my grandmother's family history. I know her daddy was a traveling musician. I know her mama lost a child. I know her roots are indigenous. I have seen pictures of her parents and her siblings, including the boy who died. I imagine her daddy with a banjo, beating up the dirt roads in Danville, Arkansas. I can write the story of his unlit life. I can tell you what I think he kept in his pockets, what he smelled like, what affections he showed his wife. No one has given me these stories. But what stories I *do* have can generate the ones I do not.

Bring the unlit parts of a story you value into the full light of your imagination. Your ancestors will be pleased.

Examples of This Archetype

In the novel *Song of Solomon* by Toni Morrison (it should be clear by now that she's my favorite writer), the character called Milkman is given stories throughout the novel by different and divergent characters in the book. Each story is an access point for Milkman. He hears stories from his mother that make him empathetic to her. He hears stories from his father that make him hold him with a wider consideration. He hears stories from his Aunt Pilate that help him understand the complexity of his familial structure and the relationships therein. And he hears stories from a young man called Guitar that give him a sense of his own manhood and how the idea of manhood is carried by other men. The novel is replete with the storytelling tradition. Each story guides Milkman, the protagonist, deeper into himself. Storytelling is like that.

Author's note: this chapter is dedicated to Opalanga Pugh and Brother Blue.

eighteen

The **Wild** Woman

She a Saturday night sweet thang, a red dress and a tall drink.

I do not want to live just one life.
I want to aim for the air
In these lungs
To distill every honeyed cell
In my body to a stingily blue-whipped sky.
I'm so Saturday night.
An open letter to longing.
What fires I've started in this coliseum heart!

The world is mostly sound bite
But I am epistles and psalms . . .
The familiarity of a wide mouth.
My teeth are gates left open for
Whatever you might leave there.
I am a yellow dahlia on an altar
Left as offering to every rugged Herculean heart.
Each day finds my hunger more pronounced
An italicized stretch of skin
Seeking the howl in hot hands.

How this flesh is the envy of God.
How we wriggle and wish in public.
Is it ridiculous to say, "I want"?

That even now the dawn in my smile
Is a letter to the world about magic

I arrive with my hands stretched out
Like starfish.
The kind of radiance that is too sudden for poetry
But I'm gon write it down anyway.
So much of us is sleep and stretch and sleep and stretch
The slow black tide of a kiss
Is a river to wade in.
I am adding up all the midnights I did not
Write love poems.
They are far away and unimportant now.
I will not waste this mouth on anything
That is not as lovely as the twirl of my skirt . . .
I am bringing you what I am.
A constitution of brown girl whimsy . . .
Eager to dance.

The Wild Woman is loose limbs and hey now! A whirling under the moon, dancing under the sun, shimmy, slip, shake, and slide-on-down woman. A flick-of-the-wrist woman. A woman built like a sugar bowl. Like a carnival. Like a kettle whistling. Like a ballroom decorated in sequins and sex. She is a "don't call me, I'll call you" woman. A woman who moves like plate tectonics. A woman made up of long nights stretched in sweat and stockings. A warm breeze woman. She would rather see your bones drain out of your body than leave you with nothing to croon about. She is the frolicking kind. The whimsical kind. The sashaying kind. The one your mama says is inappropriate. The one who does not care about being a proper anything. She knows where the party is—and it is always with *her*. Blueswoman Ida Cox captured the essence of this archetype in lyrics from her 1924 song "Wild Women Don't Have the Blues": "You never get nothing by being an angel, child. . . . Wild women are the only kind that really get by."

The Wild Woman is untamed and unowned. She will not come to you wrapped neatly in a prim and tidy package. She will not squeeze her femininity down to bite-sized bits for easy consumption. She spills out and keeps her options open. And she believes she always has options. She lives her life that way. Any antiquated ideas about marriage and family and crossing your legs at the knees is a thing she struggles to buy into. She is fiercely free and believes in every experience being luxuriant and unmitigated. She is the woman who is uninhabited. Undomesticated. Intense and uncultivated in the science of sitting pretty. No, she would rather sweat and moan and leap and squeal with the wind whipping her hair into frenzy. She would much rather rock loose her bones on a dance floor than sit safely at home.

She wants a life unharnessed. She insists on it. She caught a glimpse of her reflection and wanted to decorate it in Christmas lights. It is easy to know the Wild Woman. She is the lady you are not supposed to be if you cotton to tradition and promote standards of behavior. She is never in Sunday school. She rarely says "yes, ma'am." She has no inside voice. She is occupying her body like it's Mardi Gras. And if you're lucky, you get invited to come along.

What we find alluring and provocative about a person is oftentimes what we also find to be problematic. We like what "free" looks like on somebody until we want them to do our bidding. In those moments, how free they are is decidedly inconvenient. I have always found this to be an interesting (and ironic) response to witnessing someone do not what you want them to do, but what *they* want to do. It is all so beguiling and impressive and attractive to see a person fully and freely expressed—until we seek to hold them too tightly in our hands, to give them requirements and expectations. Then, when we are rebuffed or refused, we respond as if we have been betrayed. I would posit that much of the chagrin and disapproval that the Wild Woman meets with stems from this mechanism. "She's so free it's inspiring" met with "How dare she be so free?" She is also often confronted because she is so *confronting*. To watch her spin around a room, to watch her toss her hair and her hips, is an unwelcome demonstration for the person who will not or cannot organize around their own freedom. The Wild Woman in her strut makes the person who is trudging along more aware of how landlocked they are. It is an inconvenient reminder, one that conjures disdain if not inspiration.

The Wild Woman does what she wants to do. To do anything else feels to her like she is betraying *herself*. For her this life is made for belly laughter and risk-taking, for feeling the brushfire in the bones. She does not wish to live it any other way. It is possible she doesn't know how to live it another way. Where it takes no great effort for her to indulge herself and dip hard into experience, it requires tremendous effort for her to look like a thing described as reasonable. She is fierce in her independence. She is not interested in being manageable or controlled or subject to statutes and limitations. She is not the delicate kind. She is the blustery kind. She is a badlands woman. She loves the middle of nowhere. She loves the epicenter of everywhere.

Here again is another holding pattern that undermines patriarchal rulings as they are practiced and adjudicated in a male-dominated society and the subsequent ideas about what behaviors are permissible for women and which are not. It feels cliché to name all of the prevailing dogma that suggests that limitless sexual expression is not afforded to women. That, in fact, it is forbidden and unacceptable. The familiar messaging is that women should behave like "ladies" unless and until a man comes along seeking to get inside her flesh, at which time she should be accommodating and accepting. But she should not be over-eager. She should not enjoy it too much. She should not solicit it. She should sit coquettishly nearby and wait on a suitor—or a jackal. Either way, it ain't up to her. Not really. Not fully. The woman who seeks sexual gratification, and who may do so in the arms of as many men as she sees fit, is a scorned figure. Even in the age of video vixens and a hypersexualized representation of women in media, somehow, she is still coloring outside of the lines if she elects to drive her sex life in the direction she chooses, however she sees fit, and without the inclination to eventually see her exploits land her a husband. The schizophrenia is real. The construction of femininity, it seems, is replete with landmines. If one compares the template of the Violated Woman, who is driven to her knees and condemned when choice is removed from her with respect to sex, and the Wild Woman, who is judged and condemned for insisting that the authorship of her sex life be in her own handwriting, it is clear that if the rules of engagement follow a patriarchal model, we are damned if we do and damned if we don't. In other words, the relationship we have to our own bodies and the choices we make with respect to sex are supposed to be prescribed to us by men. When we do not adhere to these prescriptions, we are castigated for it. The Wild Woman knows what she is "supposed" to do. She simply refuses to. She is in many ways the quintessential feminist. She is the one who shakes her fist at antiquated ideas about women, challenging them, beautifully.

I have been surprised by how frequently I come back to patriarchy in writing this book. So much of who we women are and how we are moving seems to be in response to it, either in the resistance of it or the acquiescence to it. In a way, it's problematic: To be so inextricably linked with a thing that seeks to dominate you. To set up a way of being in reaction or response to something that is so inherently invalid. Something that resists balance and equity. Something that insists on authorship over everything and everyone.

And yet it also feels inevitable. Some part of what it has meant for me to be a colored girl is in reaction to what racism generates. In the same way, much of my gender politics is in response to misogyny and patriarchy. I am trying to sift through that still; it is a long and complicated road. I am not suggesting that the Wild Woman is a purely reactionary position. Not at all. But I am suggesting that she is made more *wild* in the face of oppressive systems that wish her more tame. Something in her was already predisposed to free-spiritedness, but I would posit that patriarchy pushed her into it in a much more visceral way. If patriarchy implies that her life is not without limitations, she stretches way out to be limitless. If patriarchy implies that her body is not hers more than it is someone else's—if it is, in fact, supposed to belong to "the system"—she will cut her teeth against the idea and go out of her way to demonstrate the validity of everything being in her handwriting.

The Wild Woman is going to commandeer her body the way she wants to, irrespective of tradition or thou shall nots. In fact, thou shall nots often make for a fair amount of hedonism. She is resistant to any legislation that tells her she can't eat drink and be merry. She is a pleasure seeker. Her paradigm is one that deeply believes in joy for joy's sake. She is a back road with no street signs and more than one way in—and *she* determines who is permitted access, and for how long. And they should know how to dance or at least enjoy the view.

I had a friend in school who moved this way. She was boundless and absolutely uninterested in anything that didn't look like frivolity. She frequently unhinged my jaw with her willingness to be her *own*—fully and completely and entirely her own. It made me acutely aware of how much of my life was still happening behind a locked gate. In many respects it enacted in me a very deliberate walk toward my own special brand of freedom. I was clear that it didn't have to look like her version; in fact, it was supposed to look only like *mine.*

I remember a time when she and I were walking down an alley coming from a convenience store. She was cackling and cussing and skipping over broken bottles and popping her gum, and I was just trying to keep up, grateful I was her friend and got to be so close to something so rare—and dangerous. All of a sudden she reached down into her underwear, removed her maxi pad and tossed it high into the air. It landed with a dull thud on the concrete. I was *mortified.* I mean really, really mortified. I was screeching and lambasting her for being so damn immoral, and she laughed and shouted, "I'm free, girl! This is what it looks like!" with her arms stretched out, spinning circles in the alley just laughing, laughing. After a while I was laughing too. Pretty soon my own lens stretched to accommodate what she'd done. By the end of the day, she was, it seemed to me, the freest girl I had ever seen. She paid no attention to protocol. She didn't care anything about it. She moved in her own, wild way. The version it eventually took looked like what some would define as promiscuity and that is where the conversation gets wider.

I struggle with my own internal universe as it relates to sexual freedom and what it is and what it maybe isn't. Part of the tension for me lies in the definition. Because freedom belongs to its owner, one could posit that, by its very nature, freedom resists being defined or categorized. I say my friend became "promiscuous," and that begs the question, (or at least it should), what *is* promiscuity? And by whose standards are we attempting to identify morality and immorality as it relates to what a woman does with her own body? It's dizzying for me even now. What I can tell you is that my friend was frequently engaging a plethora of men sexually. In some cases, she was uninterested in even their names. I had a tape playing in my head witnessing it that told me what she was doing was excessive. Where did I get that from? I don't know. My own virtuous mama's example? Catholic school? All of it all? In my adult life I have tried to let go of trying to be right in the conversation. I can acknowledge that I contradict myself on this issue all the time.

On the one hand, I can intellectualize that my friend (or any woman for that matter) can do whatever she wants with herself. Whatever she wants. Isn't that what freedom looks like? Isn't that the very best part of being "wild?" On the other hand, my brain always wants to seek a caveat to that conversation. One that says, yes, it is good and fine so long as the woman is not spending and spending her flesh so much that it stops being hers and starts being a thing that is participated upon. It conjures up for me dialogue around issues like prostitution. I have taken the position more than once that there is something very liberated and enterprising about the woman who recognizes that she has *resources* that some are willing to pay for, and she has the capacity to make it work to her benefit. That she knows her body is a coveted thing she can turn into a business. I know how that sounds. I expect it to be jarring. It jars me to consider it from that place, but it's worth doing so. Because the dialectic around sex work is deep. Is a prostitute dishonoring herself and her body by thinking about it and engaging it in the interest of commerce? Or is she moving outside of prescribed models of behavior and, in so doing, establishing just how free she is, how much her body really belongs to her? I vacillate between the idea that prostitution is a consequence of patriarchy and prostitution is a willful act of resistance against narrow conversations about how women should relate to sex.

I suppose the Wild Woman carries the potential for these behaviors. I am reluctant to posit that if she does so it's because she is out of balance. I haven't resolved the tension within myself. What I do know is that the Wild Woman is smoldering. You cannot put her easily out. She does what she thinks best serves her inclination to leap—period. The subject of morality and immorality are not considerations for her. Nietzsche said, "All morality is interpretation." I agree with him. And because I agree with him, I cannot attach some rigid notion of right and wrong to her. I have struggled to attach it to my*self.*

I think my understanding of the Wild Woman archetype drifts toward how she is relative to her body and her sexuality primarily because while there are other ways in which a woman can sort of dig into her "wildness," those ways often do not receive the same resistance. When a woman (in my opinion) shows up in this archetype, she is not simply refusing to get married or refusing to hold down a steady, predictable job. She is not simply refusing to stay put (like the Journey Woman). No, she is showing up in the world in a particular way that flies in the face of patriarchy, and in my mind, so much about the ethos of patriarchy is about telling women what should happen with or to their bodies and how they should respond to men. The Wild Woman knows she is not operating in conjunction with the motif of committed wife or damsel in distress (the Beggar Woman). She is about the exploration of her own desire and the authorship of her experiences, and she takes particular pleasure in subverting the narrative that she should be quaint, or quiet, or puppeteered.

If you are creating from this energy pattern, what is at the front end of it could be big feelings of boundlessness. You are excited by your own right-now everything, your own much "muchness." You are formidable in your flightiness and freedom. Your art is an extension of the exclamation *you* are. You don't need me to tell you what you already know. Art and creativity are precisely where that wildness gets to expand and plume into star shine. Let it overwhelm and stretch and dance and stretch and twirl and stretch and boom and stretch and stretch. Wild Woman, what else is there but that?

Attributes

- Feral
- Fierce
- Unbroken
- Unmanageable
- Free

Exercise for the Wild Woman

Consider this from D. H. Lawrence: "I never saw a wild thing sorry for itself. A small bird will drop frozen dead from a bough without ever having felt sorry for itself."

Use this line to build from. Build your poem from this line and this idea. Or if you like, use lines from Ida Cox's song "Wild Women Don't Have the Blues," referenced earlier. You might try building from "You never get nothin' by bein' an angel, child." Write the thunder-smack of your great big life. No prescriptions. No formulas. Just you and all that jubilee in your bones. Get it done.

Examples of This Archetype

I have had one singular person in mind while writing this chapter. In the novel *The Color Purple*, the character Shug Avery epitomizes the Wild Woman as I understand her. She had babies out of wedlock and left them with her parents so she could be out on the road singing and swinging her hips in juke joints, bedecked in red sequined dress, waving a white feather, and dripping with a lustful ooze that made men clamor and women envious. She was available to experience, was unapologetic about sex and her own sexuality, and presided over the men she interacted with, including the central character (Mister) Albert, who was such a dominating bully, an abusive figure in every other area of his life.

Her daddy was a preacher who greatly disapproved of his daughter's lifestyle, and that was the one real source of wounding for Shug. Her need for her father's affection and acceptance put a hole in her chest, but it didn't keep her from singing and dancing and traveling with an all-male band. She did what she wanted. She knew what the expectation was, and she did not concede to it. Everything about Shug Avery's experience was written and directed by Shug Avery. She was a choral applause of sensuality and recklessness.

The first time I read the novel, Shug Avery's kind of femininity looked like a treasure chest to me. I wanted to *be* Shug Avery. Sometimes, when I think about throwing caution to the wind, I still conjure her up. She knew what it meant to be buoyant and wild. Yes, wild.

nineteen

The **Whisper** Woman

Hush. Hush. Somebody's callin' my name.

Nobody knows what to call her.

She ain't easy
She ain't easy
I kept tryin' to leave her be but
She ain't easy
She ain't easy.
I say, who is this woman
Wantin' to live in the world?
She don't answer
But she don't leave
She don't leave
She don't leave

She say silence ain't nothin' but a wound if you hungry

And she hungry
She be
Slippin' in the room
Some unchiming clock
Catchin' midnight at the neck
Draggin' it down
Nobody knows what to call her
She won't answer to it no how

She ain't easy

She ain't easy

She ain't easy

I've been struggling to know who the Whisper Woman is. I have tried to write her out of this book several times. She insisted on being here, and I didn't know who she is. She would not leave me be, but I tell you what, she would not be denied either, like Jesus when the cock crowed. I talked to several people about her, trying to excavate her from my consciousness in a way that made sense, and then the truth emerged: The Whisper Woman is the risk manager. She is the thing that I created to get through the unlivable parts of my experience. I had to locate when the words *whisper woman* came into my consciousness. In other words, I had to interrogate, what was I writing when I first heard her introduce herself? What was I trying to unpack?

She first came to me in the middle of the night. She woke me up actually. The idea of her was intrusive but not mapped out. I added her to the table of contents and hoped her significance would become clear to me. When I was thinking and writing about the Violated Woman, that is when the Whisper Woman injected herself. Sitting there, trying to track her etymology and discovering that she showed up as I was preparing to write what was, for me, the most emotionally draining chapter of the book, I understand now who she is and what interest she serves.

The truth is, she is trying to serve *my* interest. At least, she believes that is what she is doing. She is the part of me that has been a part of me for a long, long time. She is the guardian at the gate, the grand inquisitor. She was born to keep me safe from memory, safe from experiences that might hurt me. She is the masonry in front of the matriarch. The one who determines how much truth I get to tell and how much I get to remember. That is who the Whisper Woman is. She is trying to supervise my level of honesty. She is not in love with the idea of me playing it straight and reckoning with my own ribcage. It is interesting how things intrude. The Whisper Woman is my damn risk manager.

What is a risk manager? In the most basic sense she is making sure I am not putting my head in the lion's mouth. She is a thing of my own creation. She could not be what she is except by me. I didn't know she would show up in the writing, but it makes sense that she did. Because I also did not know I would find my own consciousness so confronting at times while drafting this book. She showed up when I was feeling particularly bombarded by my own truth. She showed up when I was preparing to dive into discussion about the Violated Woman, but she is an old acquaintance.

I think I first created her when I was seven years old. I felt profoundly unsafe—at school, in my community, with my stepfather. It was a trying time. I am not going to pretend that I can make it make sense outside of my head, but I will try. All I know is that there was a shift in me when I was a kid, one that insisted on the birth of something sterner. Something that would not mind putting its body in between the wolves and me. Something that was, in and of itself, a wolf, with teeth that did not fit in *my* mouth at that time. When I was young, I needed her to keep me safe. She was the part of my consciousness that could manage my circumstances. Her job was to do whatever she needed to do to keep me from being maimed—by my own hand or someone else's. As I was writing this book, she showed up to protect me from memory, from my own consciousness and clarity. I have been using her so long, it is hard to get her out of the way. Even when I try to quiet her instinct to act as a buffer, she refuses to let me feel certain things, refuses to let me have full access to all of my memories. She keeps certain things about me hidden from me.

Writing the Violated Woman chapter was incredibly difficult for me. I knew it would be, but there was no way to avoid it. She had to be discussed, and the only way I could do so, from an honest place, was to tear open the memories of things I have witnessed and walked through—things that almost collapsed my spine. The Whisper Woman showed up when I was pulling the scab off of memory. She showed up to hover and, I think, to thwart.

In my adult life I have seen acknowledged that there are (and were) whole volumes of memory that I discarded. Some of them have come back to me; other things remain elusive. It's interesting to see how much gatekeeping the Whisper Woman is driven to do, despite attempts I've made in recent years to walk toward the things I tucked away. I notice her when I start knuckling in around something old, something fragile, something dysfunctional, something traumatic. The more I start to unearth some of those bones, the more I feel something bear down on me to prevent it. And there are things I want to know. Not in the interest of retraumatizing myself, but in the interest of reassembling myself, or perhaps *fully* assembling myself. I have been able to exhume things, some things, but not everything. And because of how it sits in my body, I know it is not the work of too many years past, but rather, a concerted effort to keep me away from the memory of certain experiences I trained myself into disremembrance around. I can feel the tugging, the strong arm that keeps snatching me out of those old storyboards. I know it's the Whisper Woman doing the job I asked her to do. That is the only reason she is here at all, and she is ferocious about doing the job well.

Several years ago on Facebook, a guy I apparently went to undergrad with sent me a message. In it, he talked about how grateful he was to be able to find me and how often he thought about the good times we had, and the intense philosophizing we did, and the times he cried and was vulnerable around me, and his willingness to discuss the hardships in his life with me, and how he hadn't found as palpable a friendship since. I read his letter (and it was quite extensive), and I was dumbfounded. I had no idea who he was. I searched his photos, looking for something that would jog my memory, but nothing came. I wrote to former teammates who he referenced in his letter, asking them if they remembered him, and both of them did. They went on and on about the same "good times" he described, and they were absolutely shocked that I had no memory of him. One of them exclaimed about how close he and I were and how much time we spent together, and I could not fetch a single image out of what they offered. Not one.

I finally got the courage to ask him if he had any old photos from our days in school together, and he responded as if it was an insane inquiry. "Of course I have the pictures!" he exclaimed. "You don't really think I would get rid of those, do you?" I was still pretending at that point that I knew who he was the way he clearly knew who I was. I asked him if he would share them with me and made up some reason as to why I did not have my own. He sent them the same day. And there I was—nineteen years old and smiling, my arm draped casually over his shoulder. There was another of us suspended in deep laughter. Picture after picture. I stared at them and tried so hard to remember this man, but I did not know who he was. Still. I had no idea.

It made me very sad. I thought about what was going on in my life at the time the pictures were taken. I was a scholarship athlete, the stakes were always high, I was unprepared for the pressure I felt, I was battling with my father, I was missing my mama, I was lost without my grandfather, my teammate and best friend and I were at odds, and I was so depressed I was suicidal. Everything, every single thing, felt like too much. *That* I remember. So many details slip by me, but I do remember the sadness I kept.

Enter the Whisper Woman. She staged a revolt against keeping that period of my life in my conscious consciousness, if that makes sense. She was going for a complete overhaul. By the time she was done, I didn't have much memory left of my days at the university. And that is not ancient history. I should not have the big gaps that I do. But I do.

I never responded to any more letters from my old college friend. It shamed me to be so absent from myself that I held no memories of what looked to be a very important connection for me at that time. I didn't know how to tell him that I didn't know who he was. I didn't know how to be honest about that without making myself sound insane or our friendship unremarkable. I wasn't comfortable with either scenario, so I was silent.

Childhood has its gaps too. Big ones. There are people and places and things I remember with absolute clarity and recognition. I go by my old neighborhood sometimes, and a house on a street in northeast Denver can bring a deluge of memory. In other cases, I can't locate anything, but something in my spirit is telling me that something happened there. Something seismic. Something weighty. In those moments I can feel the Whisper Woman slip in without saying hello. I can feel her pulling the pieces back behind a dark curtain. I can feel her kicking dust in my eye, not permitting me to see.

It is quite something to be (or to have been) divested from your own life. I understand why the Whisper Woman needed to come online when I was a child. I really do. I even understand her persistence in my life during undergrad. But now, at thirty-nine years old, when I reach my hand back into the spaces that held my young-girl self, when I try to get my mad history under one roof, she will not allow me to do it.

Maybe the Whisper Woman does not visit some people. If she shows up, then she had to have been crafted out of and responding to a need *you* had. And usually it's when you are deficient in emotional resource enough to navigate whatever is inserting itself into your life. My truth is that the Whisper Woman does not come in by accident. She needs an invitation and a job description. She will be born during real stress and trauma. She will be born in the soundless cries a dark room can invoke. She will be born fully grown with her dukes up. She will be born when you are scared you are going to die—a spiritual death, a physical death. She will be born to say no for you. She will be born to cuss and stomp for you. She will be born to throw her elbows at memory for you. She will march the way you tell her to. She will become expert at keeping you safe from things. She will be inexpert in discerning when you're tuckered out from evasion tactics and revision. She will only see you as you were when you first called her. She does not know how to be relative to what you've grown into. She is the myopic kind; you've taught her to be. She will manage the perils for you. And sometimes she regards remembering as perilous.

I did not know I would need to name her here. I really didn't. She surprised me and created stressors because she did not receive a formal invitation. But she's been doing this so long, she does not believe she needs one. She will not apologize; she will not easily leave. Not for me. Perhaps there are folks who do not feel so powerless against her, but I am not one. I am seven years old all over again when she is around. She wins most arguments.

The dissonance I feel around her these days is an agitation. Who I am as an adult, with far deeper pockets and resources and clarity, still cannot convince the Whisper Woman to stop treating me like a child, like the seven-year-old who first invited her in. I constructed a mighty fortress out of her so many years ago, and she is uninterested in cutting any bramble back so that I might *see*. In moments where I have been able to reassemble certain things from the past, it has come quite by accident or some other process that feels like counterintelligence.

For example, one of my students, Maria Ridgeway, was hit by a car in front of me. A woman was trying to make the light and hit her. She flew back in an arc and hit the street. But on the terrible moment of impact, I did not see Maria Ridgeway anymore. I saw another girl, a girl I had gone to grade school with. A girl who was hit by a car in front of me when I was a child. A girl, who unlike Maria Ridgeway, did not live. A girl named Karla Ricketts. I had forgotten about her entirely—not just the traumatic event that was her death. I had forgotten her *life*. I forgot there was ever a little girl named Karla Ricketts. I forgot that she had ever been in the world. And I had multiple interactions with her *and* went to her funeral *and* was interviewed by police as a witness after Karla was waved into the crosswalk by a woman who then ran her over, backed up her car, and ran over her again. By then the Whisper Woman was working vigilantly on my behalf. And she saw fit to bury it all, to erase Karla Ricketts from memory completely. And I am sure I must've needed to do that to cope. Even now, with all those pieces back, when I canvass everything, as much as I clamor for remembrance lately, I am grateful for the work the Whisper Woman did for me in that instance. I am certain she saved my life—or at the very least my sanity.

And that's the thing: the Whisper Woman *does* save lives. She is the fairy godmother with a razor blade under her tongue. She is borne out of the deepest parts of the psyche, where the ruling planet is self-preservation. She is all instinct and strategy and the pulpy parts of the soul. My relationship with her is one of the most committed I have ever had. She came when I called her. She moved into position. Her life is about defending and protecting me, and she will not abandon me, not for any reason. Not even if I tell her I don't want her anymore. She just grits her teeth and stays on post.

Where I have tried to find balance with the Whisper Woman is in, first, just acknowledging why she is here and thanking her for being so committed to me, and, second, trying to bring her up to speed about who I am *now*. She is stuck in who I was then. If she knew more about what I am composed of and what resources I have been able to find and integrate as an adult, she might let go of the reins a little bit. The relationship I have with the Whisper Woman, however, is not likely to ever result in divorce. Not ever. I think I can get to a place where we don't live together, where we don't speak much, but I still find value in her. Even in the moments that prove inconvenient. I appreciate her loyalty and how much she tries to protect me.

In writing this book, she peered over my shoulder to see what I was saying, what stories I was telling, how far into the rabbit hole I was seeking to go. I did not ask her to come, but I am glad she's here. She deserves a place in the work. She has kept me from being slaughtered so many times—sometimes by my own hand.

The Whisper Woman is not a walking epitaph to fallen stories or repressed memory. She is not some secret identity or imaginary friend. She is, for me—for many—all the evidence needed that the inclination to *survive* is more than an inclination. She is the evidence of will and indomitable strength. She is evidence that our internal universe is always trying to align stars in our direction. That we are built with a mechanism that wants to keep us safe. And for that, Whisper Woman, I am grateful.

Attributes

- Protector
- Overseer
- Guardian
- Watchtower
- Gatekeeper

Exercise Inspired by the Whisper Woman

This exercise is not *for* the Whisper Woman, but she inspires it. Get yourself grounded, however that looks for you. I want you to try to locate a memory that is escaping you. Something that you know you forgot. You can get a sense of the thing, but the whole picture is not available to you. Do not let it be a thing that is inconsequential, something that is elusive because of the passing of time. Try to think of a memory that you don't have the full version of because your gut tells you that some part of you is actively (and perhaps aggressively) keeping it at bay.

Go as far into that thing as you can. Scrape the dust from as much of it as you are able. Write it down. Pay attention to what is happening as you are willing yourself to *remember,* to *recall.*

What do you notice? Do you find yourself at an unlocked door? When you try to turn the knob, is there something that does not wish you to enter? Write down what that feels like.

If you discover that resistance, you can begin to have a conversation with your own risk manager. Greet the Whisper Woman. Ask her why she refuses to permit your entrance. Write down her reply. What is the risk she is trying to keep you from?

If you feel able and ready to know the thing you've forgotten, tell her that. Tell her you appreciate her. Tell her you know how valuable she is and has been to you. Tell her you are different now. Tell her you are made of much more now. Tell her she can walk with you, but that she does not have to preside over the same spaces. Tell her you want to know—you need to know.

Write down the experience of being rebuffed by your own internal something, your own Whisper Woman. Do not bludgeon yourself for the things you cannot dig up right away. They are there. They are a part of you, just as she is. Ultimately everything that is, is yours. The business of going back to fetch yourself can be taxing and tricky. The Whisper Woman is there to make sure you come out okay. But she is yours just as your memories are, so as you are digging, remember to thank her. Remember to honor her and yourself. And then gently and politely ask her to step aside.

Examples of This Archetype

The Whisper Woman is whatever you have created for yourself to assist yourself in this life. Because she is unique to you, any examples you associate with her will be unique to you too. Only you can know whom your Whisper Woman looks like. She should surely be familiar to *you*.

twenty

The **Every**woman

She is a woman built like an atlas. You cannot help but see her.

In my just-me-and-nobody-else universe . . .
In my own impromptu life . . .
I want to live each day for itself . . .
Like a string of Mardi Gras beads . . .
Not lookin' for any promises in the sky
No soon and very soon maybes no . . .
I just wanna make me a world and
Build me a bridge with no trolls underneath
When everything else is sleeping and still
I wanna work long into the night
Putting my elbows into the making of me . . .
Ever mindful of sleeping giants
I know the work will be great and terrible
Fraught with confusion and the
Shudder of uncertainty that
Softens the sterner parts of resolve and . . .
I wanna find me some songs to sing
Through the sagging shouldered moments
And be fantastically tough
Forgetting insular agony to reach
For bright orange possibilities
Found only in my smile.

This is woman's work.

We know what this world can be . . .
We whisper its magic into our
Daughter's ears at night
It is the only lullaby that matters.
Yes! We have forgotten
To be small in this thing
To be afraid in this thing
To be alone in this thing . . .
There are millions of us
Stretched across the topography of
Our own resilience
We swing our hips and
Clap our hands until the earth believes us
There is a chorus that shimmies
Under our skirts . . .

We are women.

It is written in bone and marrow that we fight.
We have taken the trenches and
Bedecked them in star shine
There are no dark places that we cannot conquer

Can you see us?

Can you see us making a world?

We have centralized our bodies into sonic boom
And deep river wailing
And sugared-over laughter
We have known the moments
When doubt is a hiss in our ear
When we do not know what words

To offer to these cosmic fights of endurance
And that is when we remember
We are women

Our bodies have shown us
All we need to know about
Magic and mountains

We are women

Can you see us?

We are everything
That is anything
About this life

You ought to see us and say amen
You ought to see us and say amen

You ought to see us . . .

You ought to see us . . .

Amen.
Amen.
Amen.

The Everywoman: She is present in every single chapter. She is the sum total. The arranged, constructed, conceived, and carried-out woman. She is the fullest expression. She is how you lie down. How you stand up. How you fight and fall apart and exclaim and leap and beg and weep and curl up and fan out and twirl about and remember the past and forget the past and honor the old ones and create life and rebel and fight and submit and conjure and be—and *be*.

The Everywoman is exactly what it looks like when we are moving fluidly through all the archetypes as opposed to obliging ourselves to one. In my mind, the Everywoman is the woman whose identity is not carved from a reactionary position. She is the one most in her body. The one who knows she has sovereignty over her life. The one who is most in balance.

She is the mindful one, the knowledgeable one. She is not a borrowed thing. Real knowledge of the self and the will to access it fully and authentically is never a borrowed thing. The Everywoman is not trying to be someone or something other than what she is, and as a result of that, she is so much. She is not asking to be herself. Her evolution is such that she is not even *trying* to be herself. She has done the work. She has peered into her flesh. She has kept time in the dark. She has engaged her personhood. She is not desiring *anything*. And this is complicated business. Because our conditioning propels us to want and to desire and to look outside of ourselves for answers. To question what we are composed of and to imagine that it is not enough. The Everywoman does not live in that space. Her life is a willful act, an act of meditation. To move like that, in a world like this, a woman has to be a cyclone. But a calm too. She is the dance between the fire and the water. She knows how to catch and release. It sounds so deceptively simple, but it is seismic. She knows the ground can bear her weight. She knows the sky is big enough to hold whatever she gives to the ethers. She cannot be unconscious. She is *aware*. And her awareness is acute.

So much of this life can feel like a rehearsal for some larger thing we are waiting for, hoping for, and in occupying our bodies in this way, we are not really occupying our lives at all. The Everywoman is in the now. She is completion. To be honest, the Everywoman challenges so much about the Western way of thinking and rationalizing. It seems to me that we are organized around two ways of being here: the "normal" way and the "abnormal" way. If you are normal, then you are able to conduct yourself according to the system's rules, or at least you can *pretend* to, and get by. "Abnormal" is a designation given to the person who does not tuck so neatly in. They are genius, or they are dullard. And even these standards are measured by a narrow system, a sliver of knowing. But the Everywoman is not a tight fit in either direction. She is simply human. Intensely human. Deeply human. *More.* She is *more.*

She is the actualized soul. I am writing this thinking, some people will say she is impossible. If she reads as impossibility to you, I would invite you to confront the *why* in that. Why is an evolved, enlightened person impossible? Why is it easier for us to integrate examples of trauma and dysfunction than to imagine a whole person? It is the very reason I almost never go to a doctor's office. It's been years and years. In fact, the last time I was in front of a physician, I was having a baby. That was four, almost five years ago. Doctors are trained to look for maladies. Wellness is not what they are looking for. The Everywoman is not something we are trained to look for, much less become. She seems idealistic because what we believe is *real* is the hurt, the ugly, the damage.

I want to be clear here, though. The Everywoman is not what you are shooting for in some prescribed sense. The whole point of being the Everywoman is to resist prescriptions and step fully into yourself in a wide and wider way. You cannot get there by attaching yourself to an image of her. You can only get there by attaching yourself to an image of *you.* This is one of the biggest disconnects I have around the dogma in Christianity. Jesus as an example is one thing, but when his image is misapplied, it becomes an image you believe you should emulate in order to "know God" or walk righteously. That is not enlightenment in my view. Enlightenment is to understand that just as Jesus had to walk through the wilderness for forty days and nights, just as he had to bear up his cross and experience crucifixion, so each of us have our own deeply personal path to walk on. I am not interested in emulating anyone. I am interested primarily in finding my own way. I am interested in my own *be*ing.

The Everywoman is interested in a *lived* experience. She does not need formulas or prescriptions. She does not need dogma or even ritual. Because ritual is a way in. But once you know the way in, once your whole life is spent on the *inside* of experience and consciousness, you do not need the ritual anymore. None of us are lacking anything. We have simply forgotten that truth. As soon as we remember, we can *be.*

Attributes

- All of it all
- Conscious

- Awake
- Centered
- Being

Exercise for the Everywoman

Write whatever you like. No rigid prescriptions have I. Write whatever is there. Don't edit it or backspace. Don't second-guess it or critique it. Don't look for a form to fit it into. Just write. Let your belly dictate the message. Keep your hand moving. Try fifteen minutes unless something else feels truer for you. Just write. Be in the writing. Write when you can feel something nudging. Write when you are ready to listen to what your consciousness may want you to awaken to. Write because you are certain that, in this moment, you are perfect. So perfect, in fact, you can hardly believe how vast and complete you are.

Write because your voice is euphonic, and how could you not? Write because even now you can hear things shifting around you to make space for how big you're getting. Write because you are the best thing about your body. Write because somebody was willing to break themselves open to get you here. Write because you could have died, but you didn't. Write because trouble don't last always. Write because you know what your tears can turn into. Write because so many came before you. Write because you have been obedient. Write because you have been resistant. Write because you are jazz. Write because you know how to be water. Write because you know how to burn to cinder. Write because you've been listening. Write because you have heard. Write because you are mountainesque. Write because you are your own. Write because you know it and will never forget it. Write because you know what it feels like to forget it. Write because you are awake. You are awake. Write it down.

Examples of This Archetype

You. Me. Us.

Because We Are So Many

I have found so much of myself in writing this, have had to travel through so many, many versions of *me* to make it true. It has been both dizzying and exhilarating. I was perpetually surprised by what was coming out of me. I was perpetually healed by what was coming out of me. This was an experiment in naming my own insides. When I write, I am calling on all of these things. I am trying to have precedence over my conditioning. I am trying to say what is underneath. It is a deep thing to move in the world as a writer. It is a deep thing to move in the world, period. When I did not know I was a writer, when I did not believe in the music of my own voice, it was a life of blue-note melody, a refrain to which I did not know the words. There was no space to dance, to sing, to discover.

I am no expert in how to exhume the words. I had to put my hands in it my own way. I had to feel the dissatisfaction of my unrecited life. I had to become a part of the *living*. The creative process is where I lose my attachments to the illusions of who I am and step into the reality of who I am. It is the one place in my life where I am the most myself. No concealment. No containment. No overemphasis. Just me engaging myself. The wild I find in my spirit is a kind of self-remembering.

I love being a woman. I love being a writer. I love all the time I get to spend in my body. I love that my children chose me to come through. I love that I get to watch them be so alchemical in their own development. I love the way they allow for my humanness. I love that I get to write about it all. In fact, every poem I write is, in one respect or another, a love poem. An ode to my open mouth. Each syllable pulls my head up from my chest. I am surprised every time writing comes from me. Every time. And it comes through me pretty easily now. The more you practice making yourself available to the words, the more you start to notice the persistent gust of wind in your chest. Most days I feel like a woman composed of labyrinths. There are so many of us left, slick-fingering our crystal ball hearts into daylight. We seem unreal. Worth a thousand red, rumbling midnights. We are supposed to condense all of this storied flesh into a flick of the wrist and a coquettish smile. That's the rumpled down, categorical business of femininity. I don't have time for any of that nonsense. The blight of the unborn mouth is a ship with neither oar nor captain.

Creation is a meditation. An offering. Something cosmic. Something permanent. It will sound blasphemous to some, but writing tells me exactly what the divine is and *where*. It is as close as I get to God awareness. I don't feel it from some far-off place. It isn't poised aloof and in the abstract. I feel it from the inside—from the center of myself. So much so, it stops being a feeling and starts being a knowing. I understand what it feels like to love so hard that something insists on being *born*. If I did not love myself, if I did not know what I am for, I couldn't write a thing.

I had ancestors whose voices were squelched and stolen. That I can speak and be fully expressed holds so much weight. I can feel those seized Africans sizzle up through me. I can feel them peeking out through the pages telling me to keep going—to write it all down. I can feel all of those long-legged women in my family's histography smiling up through me, tickled that their stories live so deliberately in me. I feel so damn *honored* to operate in the full utility of my voice. It is an *amen* every time. It is the best kind of voodoo and worship.

Listen. Somebody in my family was languishing in the belly of a ship. Somebody lay in a mishmash of broken bodies in the dark and bleeding awful on a transatlantic voyage. Somebody's sorrow was so guttural it was languageless. Somebody lost everything and everyone they ever loved. Somebody's back was split open. Somebody kept company with the dead and dying, the clinking of chains, the creaking wood, the all night howls. The terror they walked through. The terrible, terrible suffering that became muscle memory.

Somebody, whose blood moves in me, lay in the bottom of a slave ship and made the supernatural choice to *stay.* To endure. To keep their heads above their necks. To feel the lash and the branding irons and the dis-ease. To have their mother tongue pulled from their mouths. To be violated and pummeled and snatched and broken again and again and again. And I believe they made that choice because they were thinking about *me.* About us. About what might be possible if they elected to *survive.* Somebody should get to tell their story. Somebody would have to put the words back in their mouths. Somebody could resurrect all that was unsaid. Somebody should get free enough to put the flesh on the bones.

I am clear that so many did not make it. So many died along the way. Millions. Left to the biting sharks that trailed those ships. Left to the salted bone heap in the Atlantic. So many died of disease. So many jumped overboard. So many died on plantations, in sugarcane fields. So many people were lynched. So many people were burned. Tied to trees. Their bodies torn into by hunting dogs. I come from them.

And the women were pinned down and pushed through. They had children by men who reviled them. They nursed babies that grew up to revile them. I come from them. They did not die. They have breath here. My great-great-grandfather who walked the Trail of Tears—I come from him. He did not die. He has breath and *breadth* here.

I write to remind myself of these things. I write because it is given to me to speak. I write to dance on the edge of the world. A smoke stack. A deep well. A good rumble. A praise shout. Yes, praise. I write to praise this body and the way I woke up this morning. To praise the song I sang in the shower. Just praise. Praise the miracle I am and the mess I have been. Praise the language for being my familiar. Praise the woman whose skin I burst through. Praise the grandparents I had and the children I have and the people in my life who are supernatural in their affection and commitment. Praise. Praise the opening of the gate. Praise the girl I was. The one who kept too much empty. The one who looked up one day and fell in love with her*self.* Praise. Praise the forgetting of fear. Praise. Praise the becoming. Praise the journey. Praise the fight. Praise. Praise the where-withal. Praise the fleshier, wider parts of tomorrow. Praise the right-now amen that is today. Praise the riding of wind without asking permission. Praise. Praise.

Touch your mouth and say, *mine.* Touch your throat and say, *mine.* Touch your head and say, *mine.* Touch your breasts, and your back, and your hips, and your thighs, and say, *mine. Mine. Mine. Mine.* Tell your body she is holy. Tell your heart she is mighty. Not the spoils of anyone or anything. Just praise. Praise the universe in your ribcage. Praise. Praise the trench that taught you about darkness. Praise. Praise the day you danced naked in the light. Praise. Praise the laughter that lives in your belly. Praise. Praise the long, wide road of longing. Praise. Praise your bell-tinkle womb wet with smiling. Praise. Praise the gardens you can plant in your bones. Praise the bamboo your spine can become. Praise the stories you've kept and the ones you didn't. Praise the clawed-through all-day wanting. Praise the crinkled corners of unopened notebooks. Praise the day you elected to peer into them. To write. To create. To make yourself a world. Just praise.

Praise the scrap and gristle you've got. Praise your being, your becoming. Praise because nobody is you. What an awesome, wondrous thing, to be the only *you* there is in the world. Why would you ever look outside of yourself to find yourself? The most revolutionary act is to go *inside* . . . over and over again. To praise every part. The bones and the blood. The frailty. The fragility. The impossible resilience. Praise the atoms and the cells that make your body a cathedral. Praise. Praise that there is *so* much of you left. Praise. Praise the otherworldly algorithm that is your heart. Yes, especially that. Praise and praise and praise. Revolution *is* the sound of your heart still beating. So praise. Praise. Praise.

Acknowledgments

For my mama, Jacquelyn Elizabeth Benton, because you *are* the Everywoman. And for Joe Johnson, because you are missed and because you are *here*. And Byron and Christine Johnson, because you are missed and because you are *here*. And Lisa Marie Benton, who is so very necessary. And Salih, Najah, Amir, and Igi, who came through me and grow me exponentially. For Denice, who is what big love looks like, and Faatma, who is wondrous. For Neambe, whose soul work informed so many parts of this book without her even knowing it. For Mahogany Brown, whose sisterhood matters so much. And my sister Nikki, who matters, and Malecia, who matters, and Celia, who matters, and Rachel McKibbens, a bruja with wide shoulders and deep magic, who matters very much. For Chantal Pierrat, who grandly suggested that I write this book. I have known women—women who are thick with conjure and truth-telling. They are whom I go to. They show me where home is. They help me see how uncursed I am. I am so grateful. So very, very grateful. Amen.

About the Author

Dominique Christina is a writer, performer, educator, and activist. She has over ten years' experience as a licensed teacher, holding double master's degrees in education and English literature. She holds four national titles in the three years she has been competing in slam poetry, including the 2012 and 2014 Women of the World Slam Champion and 2011 National Poetry Slam Champion. She conducts performances and workshops for colleges and universities all over the country. Her work has been published in various literary journals, magazines, and anthologies, including *Alight Literary Journal, Tandem Poetry Anthology, The Dead Animal Handbook, Heart and Soul Magazine,* and *Hysteria,* and has been featured on Upworthy and the Huffington Post. Her first full-length poetry book, *The Bones, the Breaking, the Balm: A Colored Girl's Hymnal,* was released in 2014. She lives in Denver and New York City. For more, please see dominiquechristina.com.

About Sounds True

Sounds True is a multimedia publisher whose mission is to inspire and support personal transformation and spiritual awakening. Founded in 1985 and located in Boulder, Colorado, we work with many of the leading spiritual teachers, thinkers, healers, and visionary artists of our time. We strive with every title to preserve the essential "living wisdom" of the author or artist. It is our goal to create products that not only provide information to a reader or listener, but that also embody the quality of a wisdom transmission.

For those seeking genuine transformation, Sounds True is your trusted partner. At SoundsTrue.com you will find a wealth of free resources to support your journey, including exclusive weekly audio interviews, free downloads, interactive learning tools, and other special savings on all our titles.

To learn more, please visit SoundsTrue.com/freegifts or call us toll free at 800.333.9185.

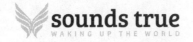